An evaluation of the relevance of corporate venture capital investment as a means for diversified high-technology concerns to sustain competitiveness

Karsten Jennisen

Bibliographic information published by the German National Library:

The German National Library lists this publication in the National Bibliography; detailed bibliographic data are available on the Internet at http://dnb.dnb.de.

ISBN: 9783867465281
This book is also available as an ebook.

Trappentreustraße 1
80339 München

Print and binding: Books on Demand GmbH, Norderstedt, Germany
Printed on acid-free paper from responsible sources.

Dissertation on the subject

An evaluation of the relevance of corporate venture capital investment as a means for diversified high-technology concerns to sustain competitiveness

written by
Karsten Jennissen
born in Cologne, Germany

at Coventry Business School, Coventry University under the supervision of Simon Horsman, and at the Business School of the University of Applied Sciences, Aachen, Germany, under the supervision of Prof. Dr. Uwe Bestmann, 1998/99.

Contents

List of abbreviations

CFD	Capability to focus development
CI	Competitive intelligence
CSE	Competitive support and education
CVC	Corporate venture capital
EIB	European Investment Bank
OSC	Organisational structures and cultures
R	Research
R&D	Research and development
SC	Shareholder communication

List of figures

List of tables

A. Introduction and methodology

US Industrial corporations have started investing in small ventures in the 1960s. After stock market declines in the 1970s, which led to exits from corporate venture capital activity, many companies such as DuPont, Monsanto, General electric, AT&T and 3M re-entered the venture capital market in the 1980s and became an important source of finance for entrepreneurs in the late 1980s and 1990s. European and Japanese firms followed US firms during the 1980s, however corporate venture capital activity has not been as frequent as in the USA. Especially European firms have been more cautious (McNally, 1997: 58-63).

Research about corporate venture capital is limited in comparison with research on venture capital in general. Usually corporate venture capital is simply mentioned within other contexts, such as interfirm collaboration, general venture capital activities or corporate new business development. Nevertheless, there is a small number of empirical studies specifically on corporate venture capital, most of which were done in the 1980s (McNally, 1997: 57-8). Recent studies by Silver (1993), Schween (1996) and McNally (1997) present an overview of the current range of corporate motivations. The objectives from the investors point of view have changed from diversification to primarily strategic concerns which is reflected in literature. However, studies do not examine whether corporate venture capital is the appropriate instrument for investors to cope with the demands of the high technology market environment which is characterised by dynamic competition and uncertainty. A further question is how CVC investment relates to the overall range of activities of investors to cope with the market environment.

This paper tries to evaluate how corporate venture capital investment can contribute to sustaining competitiveness of large high technology concerns. To obtain a means of evaluation, the issue of competitiveness firstly has to be examined in general. As the aspects that determine competitiveness cover a broad spectrum, the main part of this paper deals with the competitiveness of high technology concerns in the current market situation. Once an approach to sustaining competitiveness has been developed the following part examines in which way recent empirical data regarding corporate venture capital investment support the findings.

In the first chapter the paper deals with definitions in the context of the term technology. This is necessary because many definitions are not clear or uniform and because a common base for the paper is needed. The second part of the first chapter outlines general issues regarding high technology concerns and the market environment to clarify more specific terminology and indicate aspects that are relevant to the discussion of competitiveness.

The second chapter discusses the competitiveness of high technology concerns. In the first part competitiveness is examined with the help of a general framework developed by Feurer and Chaharbaghi (1994). Along this framework a substantial amount of secondary literature is reviewed and discussed to bring forward evidence for all aspects that influence competitiveness. In the second part of chapter two an approach to competitiveness for high technology concerns is developed by finding common elements from the discussion in the first part and by examining their characteristics.

The third chapter then looks at how corporate venture capital investment contributes to competitiveness. First the basic characteristics of corporate venture capital are outlined. Then the results of recent empirical studies are taken to examine in which way the efforts of high technology concerns to sustain competitiveness are advanced by corporate venture capital investment.

The reason why the author has chosen to rely on secondary data is twofold. Firstly, the issue of competitiveness has many facets which are far-reaching. Secondary data can provide the range needed to make informed statements. Secondly, the studies on corporate venture capital indicate that additional primary research would not be able to contribute significant new insights as to potential benefits of corporate venture capital investment.

B. Basics regarding technology and high technology concerns

I. Definitions and characteristics of technology and the technology market

1. Science and research

Contrary to what one might expect there are no generally accepted definitions of science and research. The scope of the term science varies in different languages, as described by Staal (1995:7, cited by Braun, 1998). In the English language it denotes physical, life and mathematical sciences whereas its equivalent in other languages also comprises human science, social science and natural science. Furthermore, the nature of science and its differentiation from research is not always clear. Often the terms have circular definitions (Braun, 1998: 9; Betz, 1998: 77). In the context of this paper, the term *science* shall be used for the 'knowledge base', i.e. the understanding of nature and humanity, as well as accepted methods to describe, manipulate and expand the knowledge base. Science therefore is an object which consists of a knowledge base and methods. *Research* shall be regarded as the *activity* of using scientific methods to describe, manipulate and expand the knowledge base.[1]

2. Technology

Technology, often used broadly as in 'the state of technology', has meanings ranging from the 'general level of scientific knowledge' to 'means of production' (Basadur, 1995: 4, 53). Definitions either take a more practical route in stressing the aim of technology to be 'attaining performance characteristics of products and processes' (Siemens AG Definition, cited in Braun, 1998), see technology primarily as machines (Rhodes E. and Wield D., 1994) or see it as the application of science (Layton, 1977, cited in Rhodes E. and Wield D., 1994). As a variation of the first type technology is sometimes used as a synonym for technique or

[1] These definitions are not given in the intention to clarify overlapping meanings in the general use of the terms science and research but rather to have a consistent terminology for this paper. Furthermore, the term research shall be looked at again after 'technology' has been defined.

algorithm (Basadur, 1995: 43). However, technique and technology have distinct meanings as one will see after a more accurate definition of the latter.[2]

Betz (1998: 46-7) has identified four semantic contexts of the term technology. These are

1. Technology as a generic concept, e.g. 'flight' or 'gun'
2. Technology as a system, which denotes the different configurations that are possible to achieve a generic concept, e.g. aeroplanes or helicopters achieve flight in different configurations
3. Technology as application contexts, i.e. the human context the technology system is set in, e.g. flight is used in military or in commerce
4. Technology as artefacts, i.e. actual, recognisable products and devices

One needs semantic contexts in the definition process. They do not, however, represent a viable definition in themselves, as they are still vague (e.g. what exactly constitutes a generic concept?). Moreover, from a management point of view, contexts may not prove useful.

A useful starting point is to attempt to derive the properties of technology that encompass all definitions. Betz (1998: 9) defines the three basic characteristics of technology as „the knowledge of the manipulation of nature for human purpose“,[3] i.e.

1. form of knowledge
2. manipulation of nature
3. human purpose

These elements need to be outlined in more detail.

Technological knowledge draws on the scientific knowledge base. This has been discussed to a fair extend in research (Rhodes E. and Wield D., 1994). Rhodes and Wield also find that science and technology have distinct traditions. What remains unclear, however, is the exact relation between technological knowledge and scientific knowledge, except for the presumption that knowledge flows in both directions (Layton 1971, cited in Rhodes E. and Wield D., 1994). This issue does not need to be resolved because it would lead too far in the context of this paper and it restricts the view needed for the management of change.

---

[2] The term technique will subsequently be differentiated.

[3] This is an approach similar to the second conceptual framework described by Rhodes and Wield (1994)

The fields of science technological knowledge draws on have changed in the course of time. For many industrial goods, the predominant field, even though not exclusively, has been natural science. As the trend towards more service and information in relation to all goods produced changes the way industries function, other sciences, e.g. languages and social sciences, contribute to technological knowledge as well. A typical example is software development, which not only draws on hardware specifications, but uses behavioural sciences to optimise interfaces. For technology to fulfil a human purpose in a better way a variety of sciences need to be recognised as an equally important basis.

Technology is a *general* manipulation of nature. Therefore the term technology needs to be differentiated from actual products and processes. Products most closely resemble technological artefacts as described earlier. There can be a variety of distinct products that use a common technology, i.e. technology achieves a certain functionality which in turn can be used in more than one product. For example, different cars of the same manufacturer might be based on exactly the same technologies, where only the shape of the metal, the arrangement of items and the colours are different. All technologies encompass processes which, again using Betz's semantic contexts of technology, can be regarded as systems. Processes can be broken down into two or more technologies. This also highlights the fact that the knowledge base of a certain technology may comprise knowledge bases of other technologies.

Above definitions are not satisfactory if one takes the view of the management of technology firms. In an attempt to give a definition of technology to best fulfil the purpose of this paper, one can extend Betz's three characteristics. The knowledge base of a technology cannot only incorporate *all sciences* as its foundation, but also includes *how scientific knowledge can be taken advantage of for use* as well as *knowledge about user and market needs.*[4] Technology therefore resembles a *knowledge base in the described sense* which is *particularly fit to be developed into marketable products*, or *to be licensed to others*.[5] (See figure 1.)[6]

[4] The prerequisite that a technology must be used or fulfil market needs to be successful has been recognised by Child (1987 cited by Pettigrew A. and Whipp R., 1991) and other authors (Chattel, 1998: 11). Still, market needs have commonly been overlooked in technology definitions.

[5] Mandeville's (1998: 362) definition of technology as „information applied to doing things" supports the unrestricted potential knowledge scope as a basis of technology, which is an important circumstance to remember. However it lacks differentiation to 'technique'.

[6] The author acknowledges that there are a variety of models that describe types of knowledge and processes between them in detail (e.g. Betz, 1998: 96). These views, however, are not appropriate, as they would be too stringent in this context.

Figure 1: Technology model

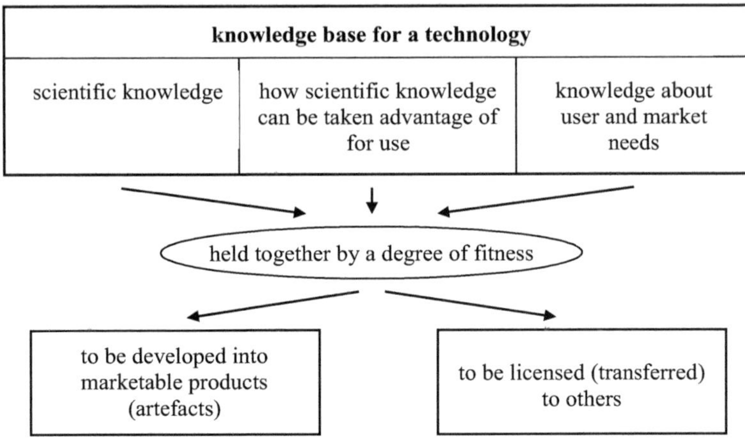

A few notes can be made regarding before-mentioned definitions. Firstly, the fact that a technology incorporates a degree of fitness for the development of marketable products is its main differentiation factor from science. Secondly, the categorisation *core technology* refers to its qualification as a generic technology. A generic technology incorporates a wide scope of development potential, i.e. further developing potential for a high variety of artefacts, for different configurations or in a diverse range of application contexts. A generic technology is created when knowledge is *significantly* expanded in either or a combination of the three types. The terms core technology and specialist technology need to be seen as relative. Not all core technologies create whole industries, as did for example the compact disc or the "von Neumann Principle" in today's computers. Nevertheless, a technology might be the core of a certain product or system range or application context.

3. Technique

As mentioned before the term technique needs to be differentiated from technology. As Braun (1997: 10) states a technique is „the knowledge and mastery of the rules and practices of an activity". Techniques can therefore be any recognisable pattern of an activity that may or may not serve a purpose and need not include the manipulation of nature.

4. Types of research

The definition of research given earlier determined the scope of research as being scientific knowledge. Opposite to other terms there are accepted categorisations of the scopes of research in literature (OECD, 1984 cited in Braun, 1997; Rhodes and Wield, 1994; Budworth, 1996). Commonly, three types of research are recognised, basic research, applied research and experimental development. The last type widens the scope of the original definition towards technological knowledge, which is already implied in the term 'development'. According to the OECD (1984, cited by Braun, 1997: 11-12) the three types are defined as follows:

Basic research is „experimental or theoretical work undertaken primarily to acquire new knowledge of the underlying foundations of phenomena and observable facts without any particular use in view.“ *Applied research* is „original investigation undertaken in order to acquire new knowledge directed primarily towards a specific practical area or objective.“ *Experimental development* is „systematic work drawing on existing knowledge gained from research or practical experience directed towards producing new materials, products and devices, to installing new processes, systems and towards substantially improving those already produced and installed.“[7]

5. Innovation

Technological innovation as defined by Betz (1998: 3) is „the invention of new technology and the development and introduction into the marketplace of products, processes, or services based on the technology“. Some authors distinguish between innovation and the market introduction of products (e.g. Shan, 1990: 131) or use innovation in the same sense as Betz speaks of invention (e.g. Leonard-Barton, 1994; Chattel, 1998). In recent literature, however, innovation is regarded as the process from invention to market introduction (Rhodes and Wield, 1994; ESRC definition, cited by Budworth, 1996). The ESRC even considers success a vital element of innovation, a point which is debatable.

Much attention has been given to invention, probably because it is the most vague element of innovation. Invention is thought of as being a certain mindset such as creativity, intuition, imagination and insight (Chattel, 1998: 11,

[7] If one were to adhere to the original definition of research, one could argue, as far as the research and development function of companies is concerned, that the scope of the 'research part' was scientific knowledge and the scope of the 'development part' was technology knowledge. Betz (1998) states that

233; McIlveen, 1994; Kuczmarski, 1996) as well as a process that requires a certain social context (McIlveen, 1994; Lowe, 1995; Kwasnicki, 1996). Kwasnicki (1996) found that invention is usually associated with individuals because it embodies an idea[8] that one person had. However, as ideas are not always generated by an individual – in a business context team work is much more likely – the relation to the individual cannot be a core element of invention.

What one can learn from studies on invention is that it is an activity requiring insight or intuition into more than one area. A new technology not only stems from new scientific knowledge, possibly from various scientific areas. It may also stem from an understanding of market needs or an understanding of the application of science and technological knowledge.[9] As the likelihood that one person has expert knowledge in all three fields that coincide to result in a new technology is small, invention will always be a mixture of insight and intuition. Moreover, there may be social contexts that favour these qualities, such as interdisciplinary teams.[10]

6. The concept of core technology

The term *core technology* has been explained earlier. If one takes the point of view of an existing business or industry, a core technology can be seen as unique to the business's or industry's products or processes.[11] One could say that the view presented earlier is ex-ante, i.e. the *potential* to be a core technology. In an ex-post view the core technology of a business or an industry is the requirement for their products and processes. In other words, a core technology is a reason why an industry exists. A business needs to have competence in that technology to operate in the specific industry.[12]

With regard to the importance a technology assumes for a business or industry, Betz (1998: 55) also introduces the term „support technology“, loosely defined as being „necessary, but not unique“. Twiss (1992: 72-3) differentiates the term further into „complementary“ and „peripheral technology“. The former is 'essential', the latter is not essential but contributes 'to the effectiveness of the

research in industry is primarily to advance technology whereas research in universities is to advance science and generic technologies.

[8] „Invention is ... an idea for a new technology“ (Betz, 1998: 4).

[9] The balance of these elements has been the object of the „technology push (research-led) or market pull (market-led)“ debate which sought to find the predominant motivator for invention and innovation. Evidence from research does not support the predominance of either direction (Rhodes, Wield 1994; Rothwell, 1994).

[10] See Ahmed (1998) for a cultural best practice study on innovative companies.

[11] Betz (1998) has used the term 'unique' to describe a core technology

business'. Betz continues saying that a technology which changes at a high rate can be called 'strategic technology'. If a strategic technology is also the core technology of an industry it can be called „pacing technology". He implies that a technology which changes at a high rate will offer many opportunities for temporary competitive advantage, i.e. competitive advantage through innovation. As he calls the so achieved competitive advantage temporary, he points out one of the most significant disadvantages of innovation, which shall be discussed in chapter two. One also has to keep in mind that a technology and the innovation thereof bases on three types of knowledge. All three bear the potential of significantly determining innovation, which can be important when competitive advantage is sought through innovation.

7. Technology S-curve and life-cycle

A commonly conceived phenomenon of core technology is that it develops in a curve pattern. (Betz, 1998: 127, 164; Twiss, 1992; Freeman, 1988; Kumar and Kumar, 1992, cited by Betz, 1998; Gold *et al.*, 1980; Rogers, 1983: 241). Researchers have found three *aspects* of technology which develop in an S-shaped curve in the course of time. These are *technology diffusion*, *technology substitution* and *technology performance*. The diffusion of technology is the rate of its adoption by companies for product and process development whereas the substitution of technology is the rate of its replacement in products or processes by a new technology. The performance of technology, also called technology progress, expresses the efficiency and effectiveness with regard to its functionality as it develops in the course of time.

Diffusion, substitution and performance are measures used in technology forecasting.[13] All three figures assume that there is a *hypothetical maximum potential* inherent in a core technology. The measures form an S-shaped curve if one depicts relative numbers with regard to the maximum. (Figure 2). One could also show growth rates, i.e. differential figures (Figure 3). As diffusion rises, more companies direct their resources towards that particular technology. With a lag after diffusion, incremental innovation raises the performance of a core technology. As the growth rates of technology performance decline the substitution growth rate reaches its peak.

[12] 'need' is meant in the sense of 'required', not as 'sufficient' to be successful

Figure 2: Diffusion, performance and substitution, relative to potential maximum

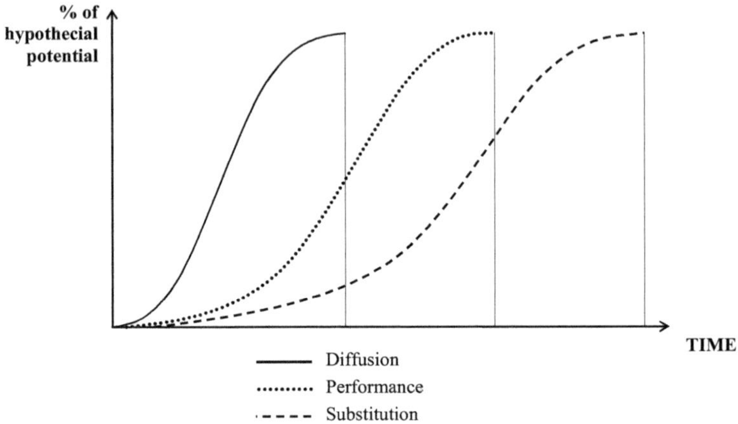

Source: adapted from Betz (1998: 127, 164)

Figure 3: Diffusion, performance and substitution, differential

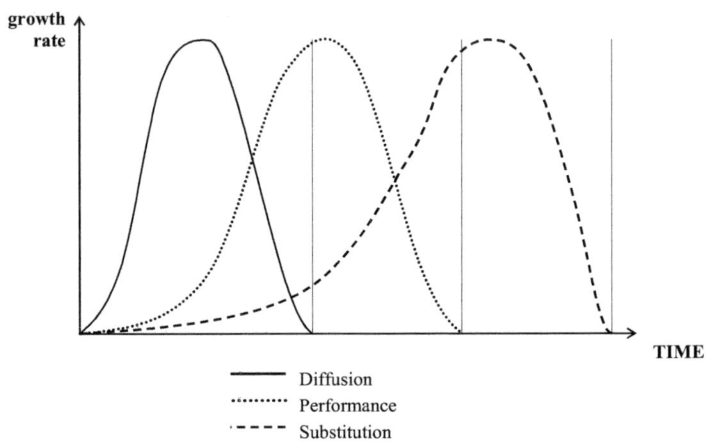

These are obviously idealised curves. Mapped curves of real cases will have altered forms. Furthermore, even though they are used for prediction purposes, unforeseen innovations – particularly radical ones – can make a technology

[13] Betz (1998: 172) uses the example of IC chip density and maps the S-curve to forecast performance development and maximum.

obsolete before its forecasted time or alter the path in other ways. S-curves do however provide the basis for empirical research which tries to depict ex-post graphs of particular technologies.[14]

In an extension of these models, Betz (1998) and others (Matsuyama, 1999) have postulated that incremental innovations circle around application and products, first. After some time the significance of incremental process innovations rises above application and product innovations (Figure 4). Betz (1998) also describes that the number of companies in markets rises sharply with high incremental application innovation and decreases when incremental process innovations start to dominate. He implies that competition becomes fiercer which results in the reduction of the number of companies as the application context of a technology matures. Furthermore, process innovations may require more resources, i.e. economies of scale, or specialised competence than initial application innovations. All models combined result in the technology life-cycle that shows the market volume of the industry of a core technology (Figure 5).

Figure 4: Incremental application – product and process innovations, differential

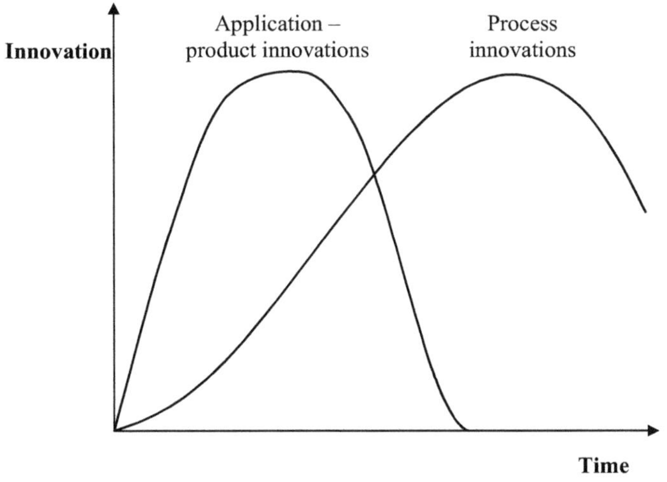

Source: adapted from Betz (1998: 60)

[14] For examples see Freeman (1988)

Figure 5: Core technology life-cycle and its industry

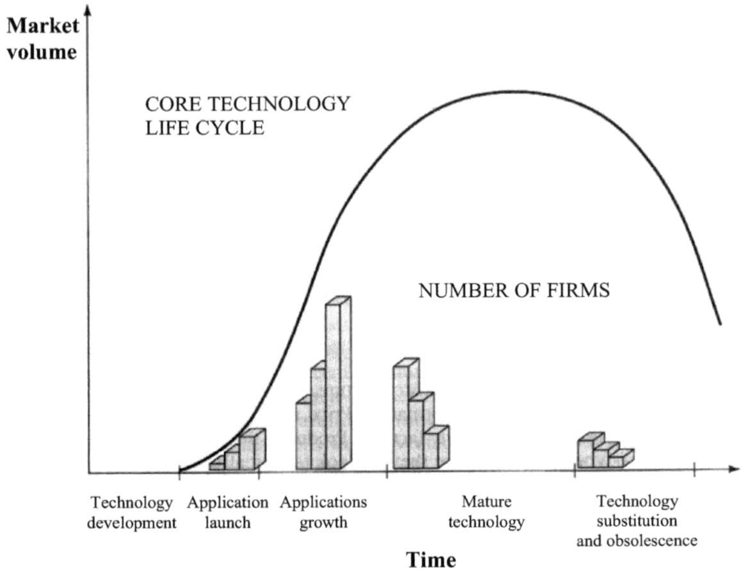

Source: Betz (1998: 63)

8. Technology intensity

The terms „high technology" or „high-tech" as well as „medium technology" and „low technology" are frequently used. Many times, however, they are simply intended as specifying particular industry sectors without evidence of why the given sector is classified as high, medium or low technology (examples: Pinnington and Haslop, 1995; Schween, 1996).

Common characterisations usually incorporate only some aspects of technology intensity. Pinnington and Haslop merely state that high technology companies are characterised by comparatively shorter product life cycles than medium-to-low-technology companies. Gerke and Grupp (1994, cited by Schween, 1996) argue that technology intensity can be distinguished by the percentage of research and development costs of total sales. Betz (1998) holds that industries are called high-tech if their core technology changes at a high rate. He does not comment whether performance growth rates of a core technology are high or whether core technologies are substituted quickly. The latter would result in constantly renewed technology life-cycles.

Attempting to characterise the technology intensity, one can look at several factors that have been employed in its context and analyse and how they correlate with intensity.

a) Maturity of a core technology and its industry

This represents the long term view of a core technology. After a core technology with a high potential has been innovated it is usually perceived as being higher than an already well-known one. One example for this is the difference in perception of the compact disc in the eighties and at the end of the nineties.

b) Dynamism of a core technology of industry

As said above, Betz has found out that core technologies of high-tech industries tend to change at a faster rate. This higher rate of change can be induced by larger amounts of incremental innovations or by substituting, radical innovations. To be able to compare intensities of two core technologies with regard to incremental innovations one would have to examine similar stages in the life cycles. As one cannot determine the current point in the life-cycle exactly, statements can only be restricted to observed tendencies. Likewise, substituting innovations need to be more likely or frequent than in other industries or occur at an earlier stage of the life-cycle.

c) Scientific content of the technological knowledge base

When the scientific content of the knowledge base is of considerable complexity or of considerable importance to the existence of a technology, that technology may be regarded as higher if compared with others. However, both circumstances are difficult to assess.

It has become evident that none of the above factors taken individually automatically determines the intensity of a technology. Factor (a) only holds true if a technology has a high potential of being a core technology. For example, Kodak's Advanced Photo System (APS) could be perceived as a new core technology. However, as it still has many of the properties of traditional photography systems the APS is only a larger incremental process innovation of parts of the technological system. Conventional photography is a relatively mature technology. Therefore the APS is not perceived as being high technology. Digital photography, on the other hand, is a completely new core technology. It has at least the same artefact, application and systems potential as traditional photography technology and is perceived as high-tech.

Factors (b) and (c) are not unambiguous, either. Factor (b) does not hold true for completely new core technologies, even though they would be high-tech according to factor (a) or factor (c). Their innovation rate may not be high due to patents or similar protection or because competitors have not had enough time to focus their efforts, yet. This characteristic also is reflected in the S-shape of the core technology performance curve. Due to the fact that the circumstances of factor (c) are difficult to appraise its relevance should be regarded as limited.

To determine the characteristics of technology intensity one also has to outline the correlation of the above factors. Furthermore, while assessing the relevance and weighting the factors one should in particular consider Betz's primary characteristic of 'pace of innovation'.

Concerning high technologies one can say that factor (a), similar to factor (c), suggests the *likeliness* of high rates of innovation as proposed by technology S-curves, whereas factor (b) demands them. Furthermore, factor (c) has some correlation with factor (a). Scientific knowledge tends to be of high relevance when it is newly discovered.

Concerning medium technology according to factor (a) one can assume that its application contexts have widely been set and innovations are primarily incremental and process oriented. Factors (b) and (c) are not inconsistent with factor (a). Factor (c) adds that the knowledge base behind the technology can be learned more easily by market participants.

Low technologies are characterised by a slowed pace of innovation according to factor (b). Factor (a) proposes that the technology has been substituted to a high degree which is not necessarily in line with factor (b). Factor (c) assumes that learning the knowledge base behind the technology is relatively easy. Therefore, one can conclude in accordance with both factors (a) and (b) that the technology need not be innovated, as it is either obsolete or cannot be optimised further.

Once the characteristics of technology intensity have been decided on, one can observe that certain technology systems use a wide range of other technologies which would be classified differently according to factors (a), (b) and (c). A good example is the car which uses high-tech components (e.g. traction control, navigation systems) and medium-tech components (e.g. exhaust system, wheels). One can say that the perceived relevance of each category of components determines the perceived category of the whole product or process. High-tech components of the average car are not as significant for its existence, e.g. functionality, as to classify the technology system 'car' as high technology.

As a result, one can say that high technologies incorporate a likeliness of high rates of innovation. Medium technologies are primarily subject to process innovations within given application contexts. Low technologies are innovated at a low rate because they have been developed close to their performance maximum or they have been substituted. The perceived relevance of components in each intensity class determines the perceived intensity of a process or system.

9. Customers

In the current business world the customer is generally regarded as being the overall guiding element. This not only holds true in mature markets where a large portion of competition is based on product attributes and marketing support services.[15] Emerging markets and fast growing markets usually become competitive at a very early time in addition to the fact that they may have been based on a specific customer need from the start.

Customers of technology fall into either of three categories. Firstly, at the various stages of the production of a good, businesses are customers in their acquisition of technical components that are to be modified or reassembled. At later stages of the industry value chain businesses buy technologies for trading purposes. Technologies in the above sense are not only physical goods of various technological complexity but also technology in the form of licenses or other types of transfer.[16] The first group therefore consists of organisational component or trade buyers where technology has the characteristics of a current asset.

Secondly, businesses buy technology either as a production, as a logistics or as an administration asset. Mentioned purposes are meant in a general sense, e.g. production is used in the broadest sense of creating value, e.g. the architect who uses the latest CAD system in the design process or companies who use machines for service purposes would be regarded as having bought technology for

[15] Terms described by Kotler (1992)
[16] See definition of technology, section B.I.2, p. 12

production. The second group hence consists of organisational buyers where technology has the characteristics of a fixed asset.

Thirdly, private persons in the economic sense of 'households' buy technology either for convenience or for leisure purposes. Here again, the term convenience is used broadly, meaning 'to make life easier', which can mean 'essential to have a decent life' or 'to nurture laziness'. (See figure 6: Customer categories)

Figure 6: Customer categories

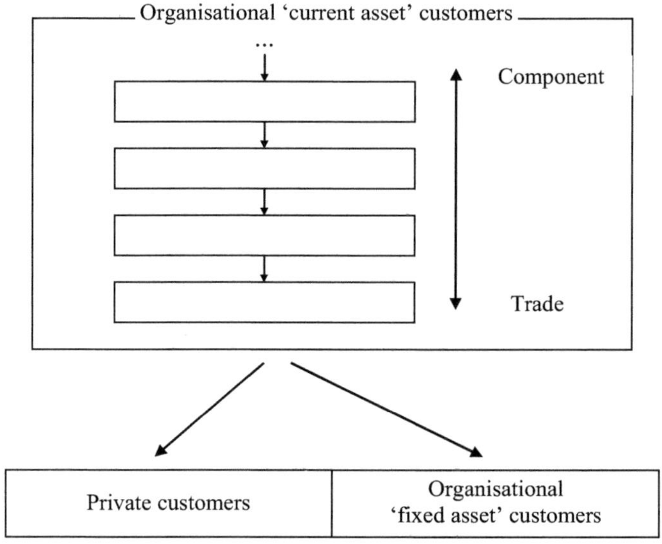

It may not always be possible to differentiate above categories clearly. Particularly the categories regarding private persons need to be seen in a socio-cultural context. For example, the television set may be regarded as 'leisure' because of its entertainment content, but it can be 'convenience' in the case of TV shopping. This socio-cultural context is subject to change in the course of time. Currently the 'leisure' view regarding TVs prevails whereas in the years to come this might change.

The *difference in use or purpose* of the acquisition of technology is relevant because of several reasons. It not only indicates certain needs regarding supply but it also sets the framework within which product development and marketing takes place.[17] All of these factors have an impact on how competition is carried out for each customer category.

10. Technology companies

The market for technology is catered by a range of different types of companies. One can categorise firms according to different properties. Three properties which are relevant to the argumentation of the paper shall be outlined here.

a) Size

Normally sizes of companies are differentiated into *large or corporate*, *mid-sized*, and *small*. The number of employees is commonly used to differentiate companies. Definitions vary in countries according to characteristic sizes. The European investment bank (EIB) has decided on a standard definition to create a basis for regulations and monetary transfers. According to the EIB large firms are those that have more than 500 employees and fixed assets of more than EUR75m (Anon, 1993: 2896).

b) Technology scope

The technology scope denotes the number of core technologies in a company's portfolio. It can range from narrow, e.g. one core technology, to diversified, e.g. a portfolio of different core technologies. As the concept of core technology is not absolute[18] there may be difficulties in clearly determining a company's scope. The premise of the definition shall be that the company's technology scope is more diversified if the core technologies' knowledge bases are more distinct.

c) Technology intensity

The intensity of a company's technology or technologies in the sense as it has been explained above is relevant as well. If the technology scope is not narrow, the company may have a portfolio of different intensities. As different intensities inherit different risk and benefit characteristics they can be regarded as similar to investment portfolios.

---

[17] Relevant to models of buyer behaviour or of technology adoption

[18] See section B.I.6, p. 15

d) Customer structure

As a last characterisation of technology companies one can consider their customer structure. To describe the customer structure categories as explained before can be used.

Even though all configurations are possible some types are more frequent than others. As it is not the objective of the paper to examine frequencies of types, examples shall be limited to a few types that can be found in the technology market. In the high-tech field of software development one can find numerous small independent studios with a narrow scope, i.e. one application context and hardware system type, with solely organisational 'fixed asset' buyers. If software development is done as contracting, which is another frequent type, the only difference is that customers are component or trade buyers. Another type is the medium-tech mid-sized car manufacturer supplier. Car manufacturers are component buyers. This type of enterprise typically has a narrow technology scope because of specialist competence in a certain technology.

11. The field of research "management of technology"

The field of research that deals with 'managing change in technology' is generally called 'technology management' or 'management of technology'. According to Betz (1998) it has evolved from four distinct areas of research into one during the mid-eighties, when a more holistic view became necessary (see table 1). This does not mean that all major issues have successfully been dealt with. The development still exhibits highly dynamic characteristics relative to other fields of research.

Table 1: Scopes of management of technology

	Strategic Management Focus	Operations Management Focus
Macro-Level Focus	**Science and Technology Policy**	**Innovation Processes**
Micro-Level Focus	**Technology Strategy**	**Managing Engineering and R&D Activities**

Source: Betz (1998: introduction, p. "x")

The macro level focus has originated from the realisation that technological progress contributes essentially to industrial productivity and economic growth. Primary researchers have been economists, sociologists and political scientists. Researchers with a micro level focus have been primarily concerned with the management of engineering and R&D functions as well as technology strategy. The latter incorporates the topics of new high-tech ventures and internal and external technology strategy.

12. The scope of this paper

This paper, as stated in the introduction, is primarily concerned with high technology concerns. Based on the given definitions, one can say that large concerns with a diversified technology scope of primarily high technologies or a portfolio with a significant amount of high technologies will be the subject of this paper. The reasons for that lie in the fact that technology strategies play an important role in these concerns and that opportunities for crafting strategies and setting directions are diverse. Furthermore, the high technology environment inherits a high degree of change which these companies have to cope with. The argumentation will not be limited to concerns with specific customer structures even though they need to be given some further attention. This paper deals with both strategic and operational aspects of the micro-level focus, even though the emphasis lies on strategy. For purposes of simplification, above firms will be called **target firms** in the following discussion.

II. Target firms and the high technology market

This section aims at explaining facts and terms with regard to target firms and their situation in the high technology market environment. It creates the context for the subsequent discussion on competitiveness. In addition to particularly relevant market trends and general strengths and weaknesses of target firms in relation to other technology firms, the frequently used term 'window on technology' will be discussed. The chapter concludes with an explanation of the market creating potential of innovations.

1. Market trends

Firms in the technology market have to observe trends closely to assess their situation correctly. The following trends are not thought of as being exclusive. However, they resemble those that are particularly relevant to decision making in the view of the author.

1. Even though technology advancement has never been particularly linear in the long term view – often idiosyncratic events lead to innovations with lasting impacts on a wide range of technology (Schilling, 1998) – periods of incremental innovation have become shorter (Braun, 1998; Rothwell 1992, cited by Ahmed, 1998). Lemos and Porto (1998) hold that technology advancement has moved away from the evolution of machines which one could forecast to a certain degree. Moreover, the knowledge base for technologies can increasingly cover the complete range of science.[19] As the high technology market is characterised by a high likeliness of innovation a company operating in it needs to therefore take a more strategic approach in dealing with technology advancement.

2. Standeven (1993, cited by McNally, 1997) states that the resources needed for developing and launching products exceed by far those for initial research and development. For reasons of short lived technologies (Braun, 1998) the effective and efficient exploitation of the market potential of a technology is necessary for a firm to survive. Particularly the Japanese have shown to be successful in doing so (Herbig and Palumbo, 1996).

3. Braun (1998) describes a phenomenon which he calls the R&D spiral or the acceleration trap. It is based on the assumption that shortening product life cycles and the pressure to continuously innovate amplify each other. He proposes to break out of the trap by taking away some of the effort towards innovation and pursue a longer-term scope. Donath (1997) outlines the same circumstances from a marketing point of view.

---

[19] See section B.I.2, p. 10

4. Target firms have to cope with a high number of start-ups and small companies who are highly innovative (McNally, 1997). Small firms are capable of innovating a single technology with sufficient financial backing. As there are a large number of small firms operating in the technology sector, chances are high that some of them develop successful new core technologies that threaten the position of large concerns. Examples can be found in the biotechnology industry. Moreover, smaller firms that focus on the most lucrative market segments cumulatively take away market share from established corporations. Examples can be found in deregulated telecommunications markets.

Because of the significance of these trends, they must be regarded when discussing the competitiveness of target firms.

2. Strengths and weaknesses of target firms when compared with other types of technology companies

The following is merely a short description of what types of strengths and weaknesses generally are characteristics of target firms.

a. Weaknesses

Most writers recognise the lack of flexibility with target firm, i.e. their inability to quickly adjust their focus to changing environments and to achieve innovations (McNally, 1997: 21; Schween, 1996: 4). Even though the causes may vary, the main ones are rigid organisational structures, ineffective and inefficient development and managers avoiding change on a personal level (Schween, 1996: 72-3; Kuczmarski, 1996). Originally a different view had been taken by Schumpeter (1987, first published 1942) who said that target firms are innovative and flexible because of strong financial resources and the ability to diversify. As these characteristics are only part of the requirements,[20] the flexibility and ability to innovate have usually been associated with entrepreneurial activity and smaller high-tech companies (McNally, 1997).

Another problem has its roots in the characteristics of diversity and availability of resources. Target firms constantly need to optimise the use of resources and their investment portfolio which renders the question of where to direct efforts to do so important. Other types of companies have fewer resources and less freedom to focus resources and therefore less uncertainty[21] in deciding direction. Moreover, target companies cannot subject large shares of their investments to high risk and achieve high growth and returns as smaller companies, particularly start-ups. Owners of large equity stakes cannot afford to risk all of their investment. Nevertheless, the high-tech market comprises high risk that threatens current positions of target firms in similar ways as those of small high growth ventures.[22] This puts target companies in less favourable positions in the eyes of shareholders.[23]

b. Strengths

Characteristics that are the cause of weaknesses on the other hand inherit strengths. Because of their size target firms are in a position to achieve economies of scale. Furthermore, they already hold an established position and effective means of influence over the market. As Schween (1996) says, large established firms have extensive human resources, fixed assets and intangible assets, e.g. brands, supply and distribution channels and the ability to attract personnel of high potential or competence. Lastly, as said above, target firms are capable of directing investments where they are needed because resources are available and choices can be made to serve the interests of the organisation.

3. Window on technology

From technology S-curves and life-cycles which were discussed in chapter one, it becomes obvious that the timing when to engage in a technology is a point that needs to be discussed. There are two dimensions to this issue. Firstly, *when* a company should take on a technology and secondly how the company can ensure it has the *competence* to quickly develop products and processes when the optimal time of adoption has come about. The first issue has led to research on technology monitoring and forecasting (Eden and Ronen, 1993; Chen and Small, 1996; Gold et al., 1980; Lemos and Porto, 1998) and decision making. A good example for

[20] Usually they are considered to be less crucial than other elements (Schween, 1996: 71-3). See section C.III.3, p. 47 for more complex factors.
[21] However, not lower risk
[22] E.g. the energy concern RWE has recently announced that it has been successfully developing a technology to transfer data over regular electric power cables. This threatens the positions of all telecommunications concerns.
[23] See section C.II, p. 40

the latter is given by Scarso (1996)[24] (See figure 7: Timing and risk of technology adoption.)

The issue of competence has been discussed more recently. It not only has implications for research and development functions, but also for the management of company culture (Bakker *et al.*, 1994).[25] The concept of core competence stems from the tendency that technology cannot be forecasted anymore[26] and stipulates that a company must be prepared to quickly develop products and processes by taking appropriate cultural and organisational measures once it has identified a profitable technology. The cultural dimension reflects the cross-functional, integrative characteristics of innovation which have been discussed in chapter one.[27] Moreover, as the development cycle is more critical regarding resources[28] than basic and applied research, building up appropriate competencies to shorten it becomes an important task.

In an attempt to find what is necessary to prevent *technological lockout* Schilling (1998) outlines an integrative model of both dimensions, i.e. competence and timing. The concept of technological lockout is based on the assumption that during the life-cycle of a core technology *dominant designs* will emerge. A dominant design is a process or technology system that is established for a class of products, e.g. one application context. If several processes or systems compete in a market a company faces the threat of customers choosing the competitors' system. Once a dominant design is established a company may also be locked out if it is not able to or hindered from producing according to the standard. A well known example of dominant design is the VHS system where Sony experienced technological lockout with its Beta system.

Schilling (1998) suggests that a company should pay attention to a number of factors, both internal and external, such as potential complementary products, customers' expectations and attitude towards adopting a new technology, the

---

[24] Scarso uses real options to derive a decision making model. His approach collects the variables that create options and destroy options for a company when a technology is adopted. These variables cover the opportunities and threats in areas such as future growth, information, relation to company characteristics and compatibility of technology. He proposes an extended net present value, combining the traditional net present value with the net value of above options. See sections C.I, p. 34 and C.II, p. 40 for a more detailed explanation.

[25] Betz (1998: 321) states that core competencies can be found in all company functions. He thus expands the concept of core competence to being a measure of direction for competitive advantage.

[26] See section B.II.1, p. 27

[27] The cultural aspect is covered in more detail in innovation 'best-practice' research (Ahmed, 1998; Pinnington and Haslop, 1995; Kruegel and Brazeal, 1994; Lowe, 1995) and in section C.III.3, p. 47.

[28] See section B.II.1, p. 27

timing of entry as well as the companies core competencies, absorptive capacity[29] and strategies.

Generally speaking, one can say that a company has to monitor the market according to the above criteria, i.e. customers, competition and complementary technology. At the same time the company needs to build up core competencies in a portfolio of fields regarding both technology and company culture and generally needs to build up absorptive capacity. The objective is what is commonly called 'gaining a window on technology', i.e. being able to quickly develop products and systems or licensing packages when a technology which fits the company's strategy has reached the optimum point of market introduction.

Figure 7: Timing and risk of technology adoption[30]

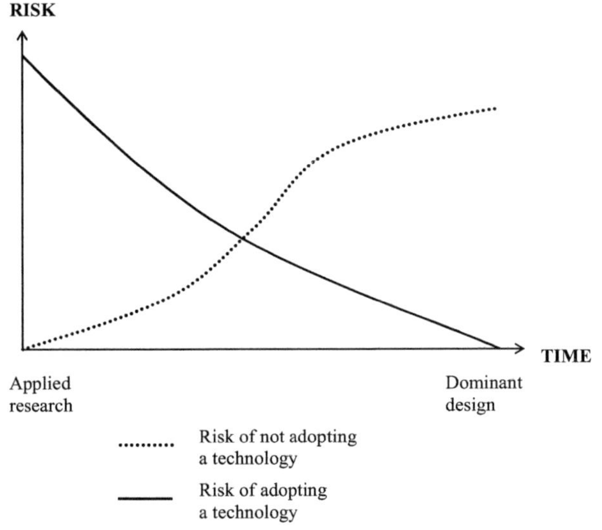

Source: adapted from Niederkofler (1989: 67, cited by Schween, 1996: 83)

Even though this figure suggests that there is a *general* optimum point of entry inherent in a technology, the term 'window on technology' must be seen from the

[29] The term absorptive capacity has been introduced by Cohen and Levinthal (1990: 128) and defined as „the ability of a firm to recognise the value of new, external information, assimilate it and apply it to commercial ends".

[30] Also see Schilling's (1998) U-shaped graph which maps likeliness of technological lockout over time. There is a high likeliness at the beginning, a high likeliness towards the end and an optimum low point in-between.

point of view of a specific company. Whether a technology at a certain time represents a window of opportunity also depends on the company's strategy and the company's current investment situation.

4. New technologies and new markets

Innovations can be of different degrees with different impacts. As described in chapter one in the context of technology life-cycles, incremental innovations further a technology's performance. New products and new processes are created. Other innovations create new core technologies. The terms 'radical' innovation (Betz, 1987) or 'fundamental' innovation (Budworth, 1996) are used to denote the latter degree of innovation. Generally, as said in chapter one regarding core technologies, degrees of innovations are not distinct but continual.

New core technologies can create new markets or even new industries (Wiandt, 1994 cited by Schween, 1996, Budworth, 1996). Therefore one can say that the more a technology, which has been innovated, is a core technology the more likely a new market will be created.

Hence, the term 'new market' if seen from a target firm's view, can be used to denote a recently created or yet to be created market segment, irrespective of any geographical considerations. One has to differentiate the move into a new geographical market, e.g. a region or a country, from the move into an existing new market segment or the creation thereof.[31] If a company is the one to create a new market it is called 'first-mover' whereas those that enter the market once it has been created are called 'followers' (Betz, 1998; Shan, 1990).

The assessment of the market value of an innovation is rather difficult (Shanklin 1983, cited by Betz, 1998: 125). Shanklin suggests that firms should not try to assess the market value, but should ensure functional flexibility of the technology when innovating. This will be dealt with in section C.III.3.

[31] Both are relevant in the strategic context of target firms.

C. Competitiveness

The high-technology industry is very likely to produce frequent incremental and radical innovations[32] which contain opportunities for temporary competitive advantage.[33] For target firms operating in the high technology field it is therefore more important to know how to *sustain competitiveness* than to achieve competitiveness.

The discussion of competitiveness will follow the basic concept outlined by Feurer and Chaharbaghi (1994). Their concept of competitiveness is useful to a certain degree because it not only takes into account the market with customers and competitors but also the shareholders. It points out conflicting elements of shareholder interests and customer interests.[34] Moreover, the concept stresses the dynamism in competitiveness.

Figure 8: Conceptual framework of competitiveness

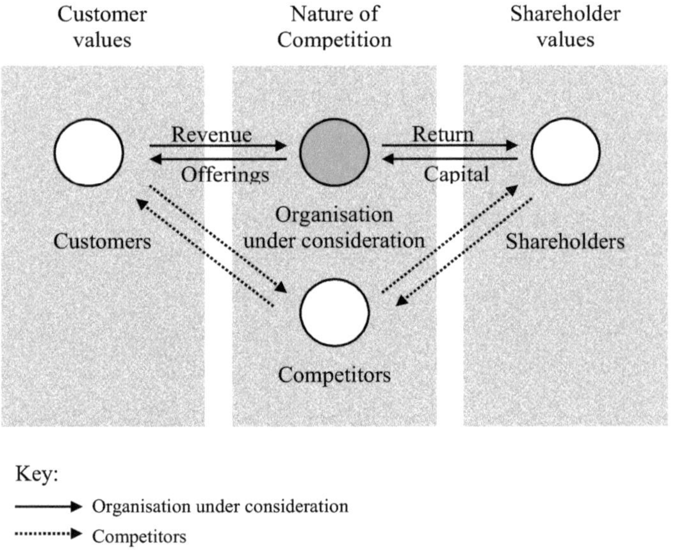

Source: Feurer and Chaharbaghi (1994: 50)

---

[32] See definition of technology intensity, section B.I.8, p. 19

[33] See section C.III.2, p. 45

[34] Their subsequent development of a holistic measure of competitiveness only leads to very limited results in the view of the author. The accumulation of results of a diverse range of highly uncertain analysis tools, which possibly even have conflicting outcomes, and their simplification to one-dimensional numbers for the sake of comparison is not of much practical value.

Feurer and Chaharbaghi (1994: 24-5) state that a firm's competitiveness is determined by the way in which „customers value the offerings and the way shareholders value the profit potential in relation to the competitors" as well as by the company's „ability to act and react within its competitive environment". The latter is determined mostly by a company's *short term and long term financial strength* and it's *infrastructure*, i.e. its technology, organisation and culture.

Figure 9: Components of competitiveness

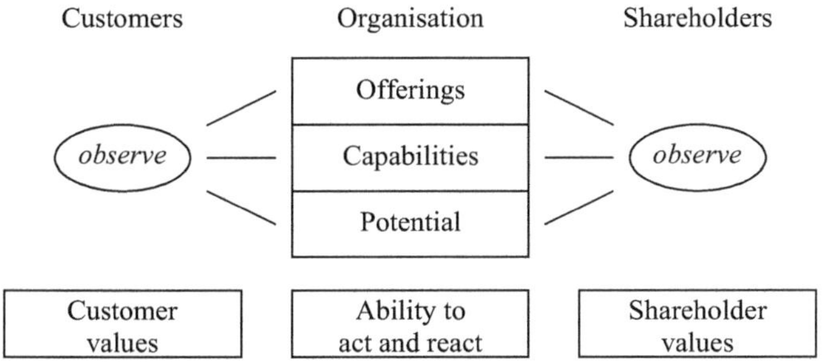

Source: Feurer and Chaharbaghi (1994: 50)

Figures 8 and 9 show the conceptual framework and the components of competitiveness according to Feurer and Chaharbaghi. They argue that within this framework, competitiveness is dynamic. From its relative nature which becomes evident in the frameworks one can thus conclude that a company must continuously change and improve above components to maintain a competitive position. In the following section each component shall be looked at in more detail.

I. Customer values

The questions that can be asked with respect to customers from the point of view of a target firm are

a) when a market for its technologies is created,

b) when it ceases to exist and

c) how these technologies need to be sold to best fulfil the customers' demand.

In order to assess the timing of adoption one can categorise customers who adopt at similar stages. The diffusion literature provides insight into the adoption behaviour with regard to time. Rogers (1983: 241) names five categories of customers, innovators, early-adopters, early majority, late majority and stragglers. One could argue that innovators and early adopters are primarily motivated by a strong interest in or need for technology or by the status or public image that its possession inherits. These customers embrace a new technology once it is available or after it has had a minimum of coverage by media. Later adopters may be more motivated by the aim of making secure investments[35] or by price considerations.

Donath (1997) states that in highly innovative environments where companies are forced to shorten their development cycle, quality and service will suffer. This leads to low customer satisfaction and loyalty and the circumstance that innovation as such replaces the fulfilment of other customer needs. According to Donath this automatically leads customers to the 'next big thing' and thus to abandon the only partially satisfactory former technology. Rothwell (1994) and Ahmed (1998) hold that technical services and other measures, which educate the customer and create links, are important characteristics of high customer value.

One can conclude from this that the number of early-adopters is higher than it would be if companies addressed customers' needs, such as quality and service, more and attempted to establish loyalty. Target firms have to consider this when they attempt to prevent technology followers from quickly lowering the target firm's customer value or when target firms follow a first-mover. In a highly innovative environment addressing customers' needs for quality and service and establishing loyalty can therefore help to lengthen technology lives and reduce the exposure to threats by innovations of competitors and entrants.

Regarding the customer types as discussed in chapter one, Sultan (1999) points out that private customers are inclined to adopt at a relatively early stage. Organisational buyers have a different motivation portfolio[36] and tend to adopt at later stages. However, in the light of Donath's (1997) 'next big thing' phenomenon and the fact that the public image factor of technology seems to have risen, organisational buyers can also be found among early adopters. However,

[35] New technologies inherit the risk of becoming obsolete quickly, see Schilling (1998)

[36] The buyer behaviour of private customers is more dominated by identity and social contexts, whereas organisational customers need to regard the objectives of the organisation. For a summary of buyer behaviour models see Meffert (1991)

one must recognise that there is a further difference between fixed asset and current asset customers. The former are least likely to quickly adopt a technology because they invest with a longer term view. Current asset customers are mainly driven by demand and only bound by contractual, availability and competence issues. They therefore can react faster than fixed asset buyers to a certain extend.

Additional consideration should be given to current asset customers of technology. Since they are part of the industry value chain, their relation to target companies is one of mutual interest. Current asset customers have to play an active role in the diffusion and market acceptance of a certain technology. They need to be regarded and influenced to the target firm's advantage and they are part of external organisational structures in the competitive environment.[37] Marketing services such as incentive schemes incorporating financial aid and logistics services as well as educational measures such as training and supply of information play an important role. To make informed decisions about actual measures and about how to achieve them, target firms must have an in-depth knowledge about competitive structures, buyers' needs as well as end-customers' needs. See sections C.III.1 and C.III.3.c for a further discussion of the matter.

1. Real option values for customers

In the section B.II.3[38] the research done by Scarso (1996) has been mentioned who discusses adoption timing with the help of real options. Most of his findings can be applied to target firms, which is the reason for it being mentioned in that context. Scarso's original intent was to describe the situation of organisational fixed asset buyers. In the customer context, they provide some insight into the buyer's decision process and can be used to find beneficial characteristics of technology.

Scarso (1996) identifies five options with values to customers that are either created or destroyed when a technology is adopted or not adopted. Their values are determined by characteristics of the technology at a given time. The *growth* option is determined by strategic future growth opportunities if a technology is adopted now. Likewise, the value of the *wait* option – which should rather be called the „not wait" option – is inversely determined by the possibility of future information that reduces uncertainty as well as the possibility of price

---

[37] External organisational structures are described in more detail in section C.III.1, p. 43
[38] Discussion regarding windows on technology, section B.II.3, p. 29

decreases. The value of the *exit* option is determined by the possibility of abandoning the technology with limited costs, the value of which is negatively related to initial and running costs and positively related to the ease of selling. The *switch* option is valued by the costs and ease of making different use of the technology. Lastly, the value of the *contract* option – somewhat awkwardly named – is negatively related to costs that occur due to a reduced use of or investment in the technology and that are not considered in the exit option, e.g. economies of scale.

As said above, Scarso's model was derived for fixed asset organisational customers. Private customers do not buy technology for the same reasons as organisational customers, as the intent of the latter is to obtain a means for competitiveness. Hence, values of options are determined by disparate sources or options have to be adapted. Generally, one can say that sources determining option values for private customers are less varied, as the impact of technology possession is less varied. Significant differences can be found with growth and switch options. Growth options for organisations can come from various sources, such as technology learning effects, i.e. opportunities from competencies, or first-mover advantages. For private customers growth options are less relevant as the strategic element is missing. Merely two sources can be identified. If technologies are modular or if they have synergies with existing goods and services, they incorporate the opportunity of a future increase in utility. Switch options are only derived from the ease of exchanging the technology for a different one. Wait, exit and contract options are similar to those for organisational buyers.

Since certain characteristics of technologies affect several options, these characteristics make a technology generally more desirable for all types of customers.[39] In particular, *modularity* and *compatibility* are desirable characteristics. If a technology is modular it can be bought and sold in small units without much effect on its utility. Modularity therefore contains future growth potential, contributes to the contract option, and potentially increases the value of the exit and wait options. Compatibility denotes how well a technology can be used with other current or forthcoming technologies as well as other goods and services. Therefore, it can be a source of the growth option, i.e. synergy, the switch option and indirectly the wait option, as uncertainty is reduced.

[39] Calculating option values requires the view of one customer at a particular time and in particular circumstances.

One more characteristic is relevant in the light of the circumstances that high innovation rates and short product life cycles lead to high average price declines in the course of time (Eden and Ronen, 1993: 345-52). As high average price declines tend to raise the importance of the wait option, price stability can be included in the generally advantageous characteristics. However, target firms only have limited influence over prices in the mid to long term view. Therefore price stability cannot be planned. Yet, there are measures to support stability. Target firms can calculate with lower prices directly after market introduction as strategic pricing or aim for strong branding. Generally, price stability may be desirable, but is difficult to achieve.

2. Competitive values

Feurer and Chaharbaghi (1994) argue that the customer values a company's offerings in a ratio of perceived benefits over price. From that they conclude that there is a dynamic threshold which separates positions of non-competitive and competitive offerings in a benefit – price array (see figure 10). The relevant characteristic of the threshold is its dynamism. When innovations happen, either along the life-cycle as incremental or substituting as radical innovations the position of the threshold changes. Benefit – price values are perceived differently in time and move continuously. Figure 11 shows how the threshold can change in the course of time. It becomes clear that innovations make higher price level positions available, however only for a limited time. As the technology life-cycle moves ahead the threshold settles back to its former slope, however at a "higher" level. This view is supported by Sultan (1999) who found that customers value innovations highest and devalue existing technologies faster over time when an innovation has been recent (note that the threshold is of less gradient in the case of innovation).

From the above considerations one can conclude that first-mover innovative activities allow relatively high prices, however only for a limited time. Whether these prices lead to high profits depends on how costly innovative activities have been. Thus the high price opportunity does not automatically lead to high profits. The threshold will settle to a configuration similar to the one before the innovation, however at a higher level, as competitors manage to further the technology life-cycle. Customers will expect a price drop or a differentiation increase from the first-mover. Where the former is not possible due to high innovation costs the first-mover can either innovate again, or add value with additional quality and service.[40]

Figure 10: Competitive threshold of customer values

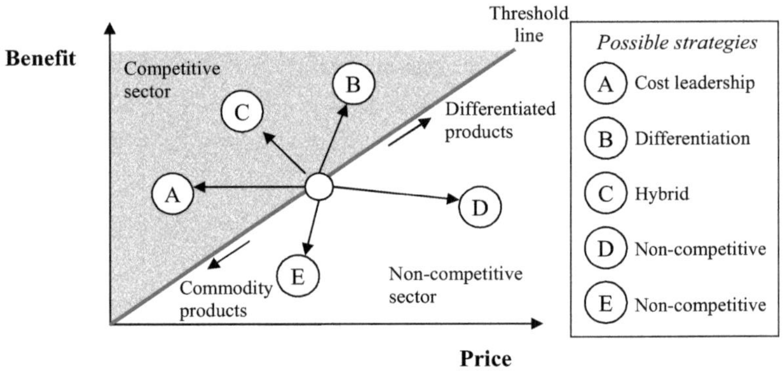

Source: Feurer and Chaharbaghi (1994: 50)

Figure 11: Dynamism of threshold with respect to innovation

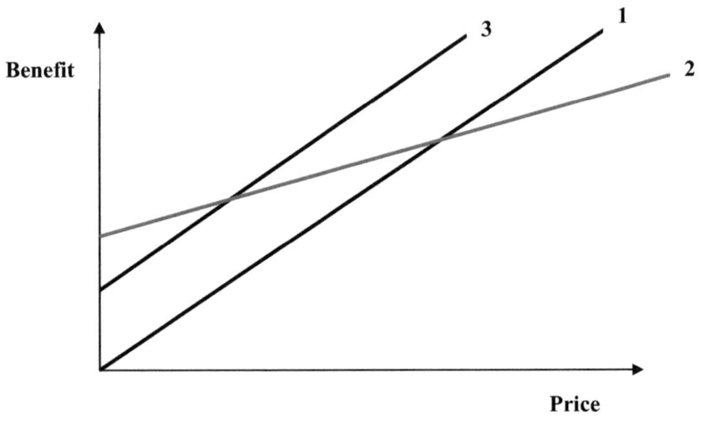

Key
1 Original threshold
2 Threshold directly after innovation
3 Threshold at a later stage in the technology life-cycle

Source: adapted from Feurer and Chaharbaghi (1994: 51)

[40] Followers may have already increased value in a similar way, i.e. by focusing on quality and service.

II. Shareholder values

Shareholders have preferences for certain returns and levels of risk as well as other interests. The value shareholders place on target firms, which is influenced by their preferences, determines their investment level. Investment levels of shareholders and the effort of the management to serve the interests of the shareholders influence the target firms' capital structure, dividend policy and growth strategy which in turn influences the firms' short as well as long term well-being and competitiveness. (Feurer and Chaharbaghi, 1994).

The technology industry is generally expected to have *high growth rates* (Mascitelli, 1999). Mascitelli (1999) and Budworth (1996) ascertain that this will lead shareholders to demand short-term profits. This represents a problem inasmuch as it may hinder maintaining long-term competitiveness in rapidly changing technology markets (Donath, 1997, Kandampully and Duddy, 1999, Matsuyama, 1999, Solomon, 1993).

Feurer and Chaharbaghi's model shows that high pressure for continuously short term profits is likely to eventually lead to measures that result in a reduction in customer value. High short term profits can only be maintained by target firms if they continue to operate from a monopoly type position.[41] In order to maintain such a position continuously the company must create barriers to the entry of competitors. As these barriers cannot be kept up indefinitely, e.g. patents are time limited or innovations may lead to technology substitution, the company will have to innovate in recurring intervals. However, as the success of innovation can depend on random or idiosyncratic events outside the company's control (Schilling, 1998), one can never be certain whether new innovations are able to revitalise a monopoly position. A failure to revitalise the monopoly position will either lead to the need to lower prices while at the same time high costs of innovation have to be recouped. This will lower shareholders' returns. If prices are kept high the customer value will drop. Both options will weaken the company's mid to long-term financial strength, hence its strength to innovate as well as to act and react quickly to changes in the competitive environment in the future.

Hence, the ability to continuously fulfil shareholder's demands for high growth rates and short term profits depends on the target firm's ability to innovate

---

[41] See section C.III.2, p. 45

with similarly high success in frequent intervals. These intervals are determined by technology life-cycles and barriers to market entry. As all firms strive to put themselves in competitive positions from the shareholder's view, innovation frequencies are continuously increased. The dynamic process of pushing back into competitive positions by creating substituting innovations is one significant factor contributing to the acceleration trap phenomenon as described by Braun (1998).

If however the natures of shareholder and customer values were wholly exclusive, compromises would only result in lose-lose situations. This in turn questions the existence of target firms in their current form altogether. Therefore there must be means of reaching a satisfactory balance between interests. Furthermore, potential shareholders have a diverse range preferences regarding risk and return as well as other interests. If shareholders with interests matching the target firms' actual needs were addressed or if current shareholders' interests were influenced, the funding required would be available.

1. Real option values for shareholders

If target firms are capable of calculating the value technologies have for them to decide whether to innovate or when to engage in an existing technology they can optimise their profits. Unfortunately calculating the exact value is not possible as the uncertainty regarding returns is too high (Budworth, 1996). In order to exactly assess the value of a technology with financial methods, one at least needs the expected returns and the standard deviation. Furthermore Budworth suggests using the Black and Scholes model for *financial options* to decide whether to engage in activities that could lead to an innovation. As these activities create the option to innovate, one can see the estimated cost of these as similar to the option price, the estimated costs of innovation once the decision is made as similar to the exercise price and the present value of the innovation as similar to the underlying asset price. For innovations both the present value and its standard deviation are usually exceedingly uncertain. Even if there is certainty to some extent, the other values as identified by Scarso (1996) and described in section C.I.1 need to be considered. In the view of the author, the results is that there are too many variables to produce an informed estimate.

Scarso's option values, however, allow target firms to attempt an assessment of the intangible and not directly related value that a technology inherits. See table 2 for value sources that are relevant to target firms.

Table 2: Real option value sources of target firms

Options' class	Sources of option values
Growth	Learning processes, first-mover advantages, synergetic effects
Exit	Innovation costs, investment reversibility
Wait	Possibility of future ascertaining information, uncertainty about advantages over existing technologies for customer
Contract	Economies of scale in sales needed
Switch	Transferability of technology knowledge, reusability of equipment for development and production

Source: adapted from Scarso (1996: 43)

It is important to note that the above table would only be complete if value sources for the *customer* were included as they determine in part the target firm's potential profitability. Furthermore, the identified characteristics of modularity and compatibility directly or indirectly influence the firm's option values in a similar way as they did for the customer. Compatibility influences the firm's switch and growth option value and possibly the wait option. Modularity influences the firm's growth and possibly the switch option value.[42]

2. Relation of customer and shareholder values

These values can stem from both long-term and short term effects. On the one hand, both modularity and compatibility with current technology support quick diffusion. On the other hand, modularity and the likeliness of future compatibility increase the likeliness of longevity and contain growth potential. Therefore short term profitability and customer values are not entirely exclusive. Generally, one can say that pressure from shareholders for short term profits can only be conformed to as it does not endanger target firms' long-term competitiveness.[43] Therefore a thorough assessment of technology option values is necessary to create an investment portfolio that ensures both.

[42] Modularity of technology can increase the reusability of development and production equipment.
[43] See Chaharbaghi and Lynch (1999). They propose to differentiate between strategic advantage and competitive advantage. Competitive advantage determines current competitiveness and strategic advantage determines how firms can renew their competitiveness in the future.

III. The ability to act and react and the dynamism of the competitive environment

The third element of competitiveness according to Feurer and Chaharbaghi (1994) is the company's ability to act and react in its competitive environment. Hence, factors that influence (1) the company's ability to act and react (2) and the dynamism of the competitive environment, which are (a) initiated by the company or (b) initiated by the competitive environment need to be discussed.

1. External organisational structures

The term external organisational structures denotes relations and interdependencies between firms, either directly in inter-firm collaboration as comprehensively described by McNally (1997), or indirectly in form of complementary product ranges or restrictive access to technologies and other resources. Direct interdependencies can be seen as contractual, there are the same kind of opportunities and threats attached as to any kind of mutual understanding.[44] Direct interdependencies stabilise certain parts of the competitive environment for a limited period, both positively and negatively for the target firm and can limit its ability to act and react. Indirect interdependencies, even though the company may not have played a determining part, can have the same kind of stabilising impact on the competitive situation, e.g. as in the case of technological lockout as described by Schilling (1998).

McNally (1997) summarises traditional reasoning behind inter-firm collaboration as being of either of three kinds, i.e. as either based on transaction cost theory,[45] strategic behaviour theory or resource dependence theory. Transaction cost theory explains that the primary reason for collaborations and also for organisational structures is the aim to *minimise risk and uncertainty*. Risk and uncertainty induce costs, the reduction of which increases economic efficiency. Strategic behaviour theory postulates that organisations strive to improve their *competitive position*. The aim is to increase the firm's control and profitability and hence its effectiveness. Resource dependence theory explains that organisations seek to *control their environment*. The aim is to increase power to

[44] McNally (1997) distinguishes between contractual equity, contractual non-equity and informal collaboration types. As informal collaboration, such as tacit understanding or forms of non-contractual customer-supplier links have a similar strategic direction as contractual collaborations they will not be differentiated in this paper.
[45] Originated by Williamson (1975)

increase effectiveness. Researchers have found that these theories are not exclusive when explaining inter-firm collaboration. Rather a combination of the three, with varying relevance of the three aims, needs to be taken into consideration (Ahern, 1993, cited by McNally, 1997; Hodgson, 1998).[46]

For target firms, specific benefits of inter-firm collaboration can be a widened scope of *competitive monitoring, blocking and influencing*, e.g. in order to develop industry standards, and *risk sharing* via diversification or economies of scale. The *pooling of complementary assets*, recognised as a particular important objective of collaboration (McNally, 1997) can have a variety of benefits, as a result of the variety of assets firms have. Benefits include access to geographical markets as well as to technologies which in turn can have the benefit of access to knowledge bases or to market segments. One benefit which is not recognised often, but of particular importance to target firms, is the transfer of corporate culture, i.e. successful management and staff expertise as well as organisational structure and values.

By collaborating, vertical integration – downstream as indicated in the section C.I and upstream – or complementary horizontal integration[47] can be achieved with *less investment* and *more flexibility*. This is particularly important in the technology market, where risk reduction and quick adaptation to change is important. Vertical and complementary horizontal integration can speed technology diffusion which can be important to first movers (Schilling, 1998) and followers (Shan, 1990). One example is giving favourable terms to and contracting complementary producers to bind them to the company's technology. According to Schilling (1998), this is important if a technology is of limited use without complementary products, e.g proprietary hardware, which requires specialist software, such as game consoles.[48] Being able to push the diffusion of technology if necessary is more important than actually doing so, as being able to *time* diffusion is crucial to success.[49]

[46] It is not the objective of this paper to explain theories and research on collaboration in detail. There is a wide range of literature on alliances and other forms of collaboration. McNally (1997) is a good starting point for further review.
[47] Firms can be characterised as complementary in any of their functions or because of just one particular set of complementary assets, even if their product ranges are largely similar.
[48] Schilling (1998) describes such strategies as particularly relevant to all technologies with 'increased returns to adoption', i.e. when the utility of a technology for the customer increases faster than the increase of the installed base. The phenomenon is also called 'network externalities'. Learning curves furthered by feedback from users and by reinvested returns represent medium network externalities. High network externalities come about via an large number of potential complementary products.
[49] See section B.II.3, p. 29

The main disadvantage of inter-firm collaboration is that a company is bound to specific partners for a certain time. If the collaboration is not beneficial anymore due to a change in the competitive environment, the firm can be excluded from establishing more favourable ties, or simply has resources tied that could be used otherwise.[50]

One can therefore say that agreements to co-operate have to be initiated with having as much information as possible. The target firm should direct considerable efforts towards intelligence regarding the competitive environment and customer value. Moreover, once a collaboration is decided on, the target firm has to exercise the power and control available over partners and expressly focus on optimising the effectiveness and efficiency of the collaboration. Due to the dynamism of the competitive environment target firms have to re-evaluate their current collaboration efforts regularly on the basis of new information.

Indirect interdependencies are similar in the sense that they determine access to resources, such as technologies, via patents or policies of companies. Indirect interdependencies also determine influence over vertical and horizontal support which has been described above as being of high relevance. The difference is that the target firm lacks control over the dependencies. It is therefore more important to be able to detect these at an early stage and to be able to evaluate them. Continuous monitoring of the competitive environment and customer values is therefore needed in the context of indirect interdependencies as well. Once indirect interdependencies are found and assessed positive ones can be strengthened and taken advantage of whereas negative ones may need to be countered, e.g. by originating collaboration.[51]

2. Monopoly effect of innovation

Innovations have considerable impact on the dynamism of the competitive environment. Incremental innovations raise the benefits for the customer and hence the customer value of innovating firms. This may enable these firms to charge higher prices. Furthermore, if competitors do not raise the customer value as well, their position may become non-competitive. Innovations of higher

[50] The worst case scenario is technological lockout.

[51] Ways to counter threatening indirect interdependencies are individual to target firms. Because of their size, target firms usually have the resources to take appropriate measures. Therefore the crucial point is evaluating which direction to take. The assessment of the competitive environment and customer values should allow target firms to make informed decisions.

degrees can create new market segments.[52] As the one target firm that has just created the new market with its innovation does not have any direct competitors in that segment, it has a quasi monopoly position.[53]

In both cases, the newly acquired position is of temporary nature. If competitors find themselves in a non-competitive position they will try to raise their customer value as a reaction. They need not necessarily innovate their technology to achieve this.[54] Hence innovation does not always cause new innovation. If, however, a new market has been created followers will try to gain access to the market and innovate by improving the new technology. See figure 12 which is an adaptation of figure 11.

Figure 12: First-movers and followers

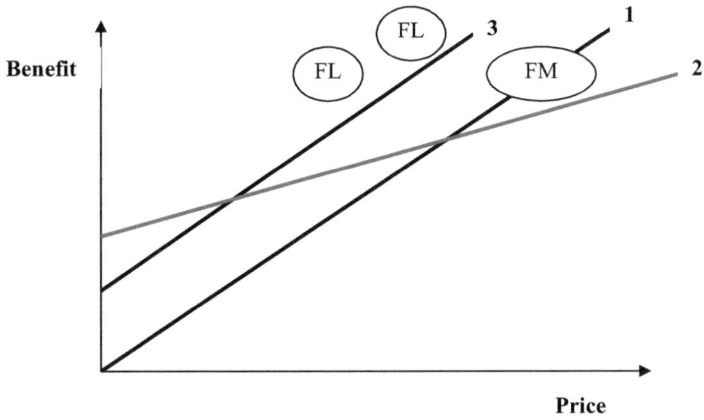

Key

1 Original threshold — FM First-mover
2 Threshold directly after innovation — FL Follower
3 Threshold at a later stage in the technology life-cycle

Source: adapted from Feurer and Chaharbaghi (1994: 51)

A target firm's customer and shareholder value is relatively high in a monopoly position. Due to the short term nature of monopoly positions target firms have to make use of their position effectively and efficiently. As high innovation costs

[52] See section B.II.4, p. 32
[53] See section C.I.2, p. 38
[54] See section C.III.3.d, p. 51

reverse the positive effect of high prices it is important to limit development costs.[55] Furthermore target firms should take early measures to raise their customer value further to lengthen the period of lead on their competitors, e.g. by increasing quality and service. In newly created markets it is particularly important to anticipate competitors' moves and customer values in order to learn how to improve the technology.

3. Innovation and value creating business processes

a. General issues

The impact of innovations on the dynamism of the competitive environment has been discussed in the previous section. This section focuses on the micro level of innovation, i.e. the target firms' ability to innovate, as well as their ability to engage in other value creating activities. It deals with competencies in research, invention, development and sales and service activities as well as the social and organisational requirements that enable the company to act and react.

As said in chapter one, innovation covers all stages, invention, development and market introduction. The invention stage is characterised by the fact that forecasting it is difficult whereas technology development is critical with regard to time. Market introduction concerns diffusion and service efforts. One should remember that innovations represent an expansion of the existing technology knowledge base in either of the three knowledge types or a combination thereof. However, one can expand the scope of the term innovation to include delivery as it forms an integral part of a company's offering.[56] This shall be dealt with later in section C.III.3.d, p. 51.

The characterisation of invention as something that requires insight and intuition has been the objective of research examining the social context of invention. Lowe (1995) finds that invention as well as the whole innovation process rests on the basis of what he calls organisational texture, which denotes organisational structure and culture, as well as creativity and external networking. Both internal texture and external networking are required to find opportunities of how innovation can be used for the company's advancement in the competitive environment and then to channel creativity and resources towards the invention.[57]

[55] See section C.III.3.c, p. 50
[56] Different degrees of innovation are explained in section B.II.4, p. 32
[57] Innovation can be initiated by all corporate functions, as Braun (1997) states.

Ahmed (1998) points out various elements that constitute successful innovation. A company must be able to think corporate-wide, i.e. spanning structures and functions, and beyond that competitive environment-wide, have a customer orientation and a management and personnel focus. To achieve these he presupposes a basis similar Lowe's which consists of intra and inter-organisational process and communication structures (hard factors) and an entrepreneurial organisational culture (soft factors).[58]

These principles are not only relevant to innovation, even though a large portion of efforts of target firms have to serve that purpose. Hard and soft factors are generally relevant to create the flexibility necessary for being able to act and react and to create the dynamism needed for continuous improvement as postulated above. Literature on organisational learning has specifically covered this area.[59] Organisational learning assumes that effectiveness and efficiency of operational and strategic management of organisations can be improved if the organisations incorporate the means, i.e. structure and culture, that enable learning brought about by all its members in a continuous effort.

One can conclude that hard factors are to *facilitate* learning and innovation whereas soft factors are to *motivate* learning and innovation. As learning and innovation cannot come about without managerial consent, soft factors specifically incorporate the managers' task to create policies to foster and support efforts, such as reward systems. Moreover, managers must allow the staff to be heard and ideas to be considered.[60] Hence, they must 'live' a learning culture in addition to fostering it.

It has also been found that not only organisational measures but also *continuous internal research* efforts contribute to learning and innovation. The traditional view of the aim of research is that the firm is provided with ideas for inventions. Cohen and Levinthal (1990) argue that this is the less important benefit of research. They found that basic research in areas of interest to the company, even though not specifically directed towards the development of technology, builds absorptive capacity[61] which is crucial to the companies ability to act and react in the competitive environment. Hence, continuous investments in

[58] Similar views can be found in other research on innovation, such as Kruegel and Brazeal (1994).
[59] Gnyawali and Grant (1997) give an overview of some of the recent literature on organisational learning.
[60] Executives' problems with innovation has been covered in research by Kuczmarksi (1996).
[61] They argue that there is no difference whether results are publicised or kept secret.

research have cumulative effects on competencies and aim at preparing for innovation efforts.

One can therefore say that a specific objective of above factors is to build *core competencies* and *absorptive capacity*.[62] Cohen and Levinthal (1990) argue that competencies and absorptive capacity increase cumulatively with continuous efforts. If one views above factors from a risk perspective another benefit becomes evident. Hard and soft factors help to *diversify the strategic and operational risk on the level of the individual*. In the case of research, the target firm diversifies the risk of building competencies in non beneficial technologies as basic and applied research is not focused on one specific technology. Finally, above factors optimise the *continuity* in efforts to improve competitive position.

b. Development process

As said in section B.II.1, the development process requires significantly more time and resources than invention. As the whole innovation process is costly and time critical, development has to be done as effectively and efficiently as possible. Hard factors, i.e. structures, and soft factors, i.e. culture, as explained above are one element to achieve this, for development requires the knowledge and skills from a wide range of company functions as well. Yet, the specific characteristics of the development process are its *focus* on a particular technology and the *increased relevance of other external circumstances*. Increased awareness of the technology's market requirements, such as positioning and distribution, governmental and other regulations, as well as timing requirements because of competitive activity must be incorporated into the process.

To optimise the management of the development process and to ensure that all relevant information is recognised and is incorporated into the process the company needs a broader intelligence concept and rigid operations management.[63] Research by Lemos and Porto (1998) propagates a competitive intelligence approach of information gathering via a network of external sources where different company functions perform scanning and processing in their fields. In extension of their concept, one can say that intelligence information must be distributed via organisational structures and culture for target firms to be able to incorporate it into the process effectively and efficiently. This *comprehensive*

[62] These terms have been discussed earlier in section B.II.3, p. 29
[63] Controlling and regular re-focusing

intelligence concept resembles Ahmed's (1998) external communication structures in being the extended part of corporate communication structures.

In particular, external intelligence is required to make *decisions* regarding the technology's *needs* in the areas of functionality, differentiation, compatibility and interfaces, and possibly aesthetics as well as *requirements* due to governmental policies, standardisation and target costs. External information should therefore cover related science and technology, standardisation and regulations, competitors, vertically and horizontally complementary businesses as well as markets and customers.

Mandeville (1998) presents a view on innovation that helps explain the importance of information gathering and communication flow which has been outlined to this point. He finds that technology incorporates a variety of knowledge and information which ranges from highly codified tangible information to highly uncodified intangible information. The latter is described as being non-linear, non-precise and from many sources, i.e. also from social contexts. He argues that new technologies tend to incorporate more intangible information than mature technologies. Hence, in order to increase the ability to innovate, the company must be able to gather, absorb and process intangible information.

The second critical element in the development process is development operations management. It consists of transferring decisions based on competitive intelligence into those organisational development processes that achieve these most efficiently. During the management of operations competitive intelligence or improvement efforts via the internal structure may result in revising decisions. Therefore, a frequent refocusing is necessary to direct efforts to the those aspects of development that require most attention.

c. Additional considerations to raise the customer value

In section C.I.1 on real option values for customers the author pointed out that modularity as well as current and future compatibility are main characteristics that significantly raise customer value. In order to assess a technology's *compatibility* or to innovate compatible technology target firms need knowledge in several areas. In particular, target firms need to know

- what the characteristics and interfaces of the customers' current technologies are,

- where exactly the technology in question would fit in – or could fit in the future – with other technology, i.e. knowledge about usage and user behaviour, synergies and network externalities,[64]
- and knowledge about whether technologies can be made (more) compatible according to (a) and (b) by innovation and how to achieve these aims.

In order to create *modular* technologies, target firms' competence must be high in the respective field of technology, in particular how customer utility can be kept at an accepted level even though the amount of technology is relatively small. This in turn requires particular knowledge about the scope of the technology's purpose and of usage behaviour. Sources for technology option value go beyond those inherent in compatibility and modularity. Therefore the company must be able to assess all *other sources*, be able to make statements about their relevance and determine whether values can be improved.

If a target firm aims to achieve all of the above, it needs in-depth customer and market intelligence of a wide scope. Intelligence measures have to go beyond conventional market research. According to Rothwell (1994), Ahmed (1998) as well as Kandampully and Duddy (1999), target firms have to establish strong links with the customer. Product champions and technological gatekeepers[65] can maintain a good relationship with customers, gather and filter information and feedback and supervise how the intelligence is incorporated into innovation activities.

Values are determined by how the customer perceives them. Even if technologies are innovated with above considerations in mind, customers might not adopt the technology because they do not have the information about its potential value. Therefore target firms need a customer communication concept which informs about these values and provides the service to ensure that customers obtain all of the potential value. This is particularly relevant in the case of component and trade buyers because of their role in technology diffusion.[66]

d. Market introduction and diffusion

The ability to introduce technologies and actual products, processes and services to the market and diffuse them firstly depends on how well they have been

[64] See footnote 48, p. 44

[65] Also see Twiss (1992: 95).

developed with customer value in mind. In addition to what has been said in this section there are other ways with regard to diffusion to create value or facilitate diffusion.

As has been explained in section C.III.1, target firms must engage in collaboration and make effective use of indirect interdependencies to obtain a higher degree of control over the diffusion process. Developing technologies as open systems and abstaining from patents and secrecy can be an additional measure to influence interdependencies.[67]

A measure specifically geared to customers which has recently been employed more frequently is penetration pricing (Schilling, 1998) up to the point of giving technology away. Revenues are generated in similar ways as is done with open systems, i.e. with the sale of complementary technologies, the gathering of information, or with advertising.[68] Additional customer value is also created when target firms innovate the delivery process because of specific knowledge about customer needs, usage and user behaviour and delivery possibilities.

Donath (1997) emphasises that customer loyalty is important in a fast changing environment. Loyalty is grounded on customer satisfaction which stems from high customer value that lasts after technologies have been purchased. One therefore has to consider that, even though high value may lead to a purchase, quickly following innovations or poor performance can lead to low satisfaction. Moreover, if target firms continuously invest in customer relations and communications, as described in the section C.III.3.c, they foster customer loyalty.[69] By establishing loyalty target firms facilitate the diffusion of future technology. As said before, having and sustaining the ability to diffuse a technology is more important than doing so.

When a target firm achieves fast diffusion, they are able to establish monopoly positions quickly and may create a dominant design. These circumstances inherit the potential for high shareholder value as described in section C.III.2. Fast diffusion also is a means of protecting oneself from technological lockout as shown in section C.III.1.

---

[66] See section C.I, p. 34

[67] The characteristics of open systems are that their specifications are readily available and their distribution enforced to encourage other firms to develop products and processes or new technologies based on the open system. Revenues are generated either by licensing fees or by alternative methods such as information gathering or sale of complementary products.

[68] Free services and software for the Internet is a typical example.

[69] See Bowden (1998) for a practical discussion measuring and influencing customer loyalty.

4. Reducing the threat by competitors' technologies

As companies innovate they alter the competitive environment and potentially threaten the competitiveness of the target firm. Both incremental innovations and radical innovations need to be reacted to.[70] Target firms are able to respond to competitors' moves either by pre-emptive or by reactive competitive re-positioning. If target firms want to act pre-emptively they have to anticipate technological development and innovative moves of competitors and new entrants. If target firms aim at reacting to competitors' moves, they must have built up the competence to quickly develop and diffuse their technology as well as the ability to add value to their technology in other ways, such as by increased quality, ease of handling, product attributes and marketing support services.

No matter which tactics is the most appropriate one for target firms in a given situation, in order to increase the ability of acting and reacting, both capabilities must be at their disposal. If pre-emptive tactics are the company's objective, quick development and diffusion capabilities are indispensable because of timing circumstances. If reactive tactics are more appropriate, anticipation may also be necessary in order to be able to react effectively and efficiently.

The anticipation of technology and competitive movements is achieved by a combination of monitoring and forecasting activities. Lemos and Porto (1998) describe how competitive intelligence can provide the information required for monitoring and forecasting. Specific tools for evaluating the information and for forecasting are also explained by Lemos and Porto (1998), such as the methods called 'scenarios' and 'technological vigil'. However, in order to make monitoring and forecasting more effective, elements of organisational hard and soft factors as described above are required to draw on the intuition and insight of all individuals of the organisation. Furthermore, research activities can contribute to knowledge that enables a company to foresee certain technological developments and subsequently movements of competitors and new entrants.

Development and Diffusion have been covered in the section before, therefore they will not be discussed in detail again. Of particular importance for reaction purposes is the company's ability to absorb technology as well as to innovate it incrementally and add value for the customer in other ways. Incremental innovation can either occur in the application or process context.

---

[70] See section B.II.4, p. 32

Incremental innovation in the *application context* and other *value adding activities regarding product attributes and marketing support services* require additional intelligence regarding markets and customers. Incremental innovation in the *process context* and *value adding activities regarding quality* require additional development capabilities in process optimising, quality focus and cost economising. In any case, the target firms' innovation ability needs to be developed as described in section C.III.3.

As said above, it has to be understood that pre-emptive and reactive tactics do not exclude each other. As flexibility is always necessary and above capabilities are interdependent, a certain level of all competencies needs to be present. Obviously, managing them is rather difficult. That is why a comprehensive intelligence concept and organisational hard and soft factors are important.

5. Dealing with shareholder pressure

In order to lessen pressure from shareholders for certain risk and return portfolios and policies that hurt target firms' future competitiveness target firms have to engage in effective shareholder communication. The goal of communication measures is to create an environment that successfully develops, nurtures and maintains the relationship with shareholders in order to obtain support for those measures that ensure target firms' long-term competitiveness (Kandampully and Duddy, 1999).

According to Wheeler and Sillanpää (1998) empirical evidence shows that those companies which successfully include shareholders in their communication concept by listening, processing and responding positively to their concerns are more successful in the mid to long term than others. Wheeler and Sillanpää also point out that new technologies create new means of communication at lower costs and thus facilitate such an integrative communication concept. It is therefore necessary that target firms plan and integrate shareholder communication to obtain support from shareholders as well as to attract those shareholders that have preferences matching those needed by the company in given circumstances.

IV. Developing a competitiveness approach for target firms

The discussion on how target firms can stay competitive has been developed with the help of the framework suggested by Feurer and Chaharbaghi (1994). Their assumption has been that both customer value and shareholder value determine a company's financial strength and therefore influence its ability to act and react in the competitive environment. As however target firms must be able to act and react flexibly in the competitive environment to ensure that customer and shareholder value stay high it is crucial that target firms make take all measures necessary to ensure long term competitiveness. If customer value and shareholder value are high compared with its competitors' values a company is currently competitive.

Hence, one needs to look at both the target firm's ability to be competitive and the ability to stay competitive in the future. Charharbaghi and Lynch (1999) have taken into account both dimensions and called the latter *strategic advantage*, whereas the commonly known term *competitive advantage* is applied to achieving current competitiveness.

With regard to target firms, it has been said that they lack flexibility to a certain degree. Therefore a large portion of efforts should be directed towards achieving and maintaining flexibility. If a target firm is flexible in its strategies and operations and at the same time employs a comprehensive intelligence and communication concept, it is able to steer its efforts to the direction which promises competitive advantage in the currently given circumstances of the competitive environment.

In the discussion on competitiveness, certain elements have been mentioned repeatedly or emphasised as essential in different contexts. These elements have furthermore been described as to sustain competitiveness. In literature they are usually examined individually or in a subset and not necessarily from the point of view of target firms. As has become evident in the preceding discussion, that means of staying competitive have strong interdependencies and should not be seen individually.

Based on measures and objectives indicated in the discussion, the author therefore proposes that target firms should undertake investments in the following six fields which will subsequently be outlined.

- Competitive intelligence
- Competitive support and education
- Shareholder communication
- Research
- Capability to focus development
- Organisational structures and culture

The aims and objectives listed in the tables are those most directly related with the measures and activities in that particular investment. It is obvious that all investments have interdependencies of varying degrees. However, to achieve clarity about the direction and scope of the investments they need to be differentiated before interdependencies can be examined.

1. Competitive intelligence

(See table 3.)

Even though some sources suggest competitive intelligence to be learning what competitors are doing (Nerney, 1998) the information needs as outlined in the competitiveness discussion go beyond that. Therefore the term competitive intelligence is used as Lemos and Porto (1998) understand it, i.e. as gathering, absorbing and disseminating all information regarding the market. This includes competitors, potential competitors, companies with complementary offerings, customers and suppliers. Moreover, different company functions perform additional scanning and processing in their fields.

The most important issue of competitive intelligence is to know how to ensure that intelligence is disseminated to appropriate managers and personnel timely (Attaway, 1998; Lemos and Porto, 1998; Gnyawali and Grant, 1997). Competitive intelligence measures can process intelligence and make it available. However they cannot ensure that this is done as effectively and efficiently as possible. Organisational structures and culture fulfil this purpose primarily and other investments contribute as well.

Table 3: Competitive Intelligence[71]

Measures/Activities	Sources
• databank mining • regular reading of publications and press • obtaining agency reports • making possible and initiating data transfer via inter organisational information technology • regular communication through: - personal contact with scientists - formal and personal contact with other R&D departments - personal contact with other personnel of (high-) technology companies - formal and personal contact in all other functions with organisations of collaboration and indirect affiliates • supplier research • proprietary market and consumer research • feedback through Internet presence • employing product champions and technological gatekeepers • establishing databases of collected information • analysing the information with technological tools • analysing the information with competitive analysis techniques[72] • making intelligence available to all staff and frequently providing managers with briefs and reports[73]	• publications on competitors, the market and technology • popular press • scientific journals and publications • trade fairs, expositions • universities • public/private research institutions • personnel of high tech companies • standardisation institutions (e.g. IEEE, ANSI) • databases of patents • other specialised databases on technology, competitors and related companies • market intelligence databases • formal collaboration • market research agencies • consultant agencies with specific knowledge in a certain field of technology • Internet • telephone and other communication media

Objectives
• monitoring competitors' moves and external organisational structures • having information available to evaluate competitors moves and external organisational structures to decide on and have the power to take measures to counter or make use of them • having information available for negotiations on collaboration (either to initiate, re-negotiate or to terminate) and to evaluate them • detecting emerging dominant designs • gathering knowledge about standards and legal requirements • learning the characteristics of current technology regarding user behaviour, compatibility, interfaces, modularity, synergies and network externalities • regarding a specific future technology, having the information to be able to decide on functionality, differentiation, compatibility, interface needs as well modularity potential, target costs and timing restraints • learning about current delivery methods, detecting potential to modify current or to invent new methods of delivery • obtaining knowledge of production and management methods • generating knowledge to forecast technologies and evaluate them • supporting management decisions and raising information level of staff • obtaining all information as early as possible • gathering other intangible information • detecting new sources and be able to develop new measures of competitive intelligence

[71] Part of the elements listed is inspired by Lemos and Porto (1998)
[72] See Attaway (1998).
[73] For examples of reports see Attaway (1998).

2. Competitive support and education

(See table 4.)

The necessity of competitive support and educational measures has been outlined – in particular but not exclusively – in the context of increasing and communicating customer value and external organisational structures. Competitive support and education is differentiated from competitive intelligence because its main theme is exerting influence rather than gathering intelligence, even though one could argue that there are interdependencies.[74]

Table 4: Competitive Support and Education

Measures/Activities	Objectives
• employing product champions and technological gatekeepers to manage measures/activities • educational conferences, seminars and workshops with beneficiaries* • provision of technical information to beneficiaries* • provision of incentive schemes to beneficiaries* • integrative maintenance service concept • using marketing mix to communicate option values • taking an active and influential part in efforts to negotiate technology standards * beneficiaries := suppliers, complementary firms and customers, in particular final and trade customers	• ensuring that beneficiaries* know and appreciate option values • improving sales potential of trade buyers and complementary companies • raising value of wait option • establishing relationships with customers, suppliers, competitors, complementary firms • developing and nurturing loyalty of beneficiaries,* in particular of customers • influencing standardisation efforts and dominant designs • having the power to influence collaboration and other external organisational structures

3. Shareholder communication

(See table 5.)

Shareholder communication in both directions will be increasingly possible with less costs. Modern communication technology is already being used for this purpose and it incorporates possibilities of synergies with other technologies for information and knowledge management. For these reasons and because of its importance as described earlier, Wheeler and Sillanpää (1998) predict an increase in shareholder communication which results in competitive disadvantages for companies not investing in it. However, not only large amounts of minor shareholders but also few major shareholders have to be dealt with. For the latter,

[74] See section C.IV.7, p. 62

target firms must be able to provide more substantial and in-depth data in order to convince major shareholders of the firms decisions.

One aspect that may represent a problem is that giving out too much information can be disadvantageous in the competitive environment, even though more information potentially raises the shareholder value. In the view of the author, there is no general solution to this problem. However, one could argue that the ability to *evaluate* information with regard to the competitive environment positively influences the ability to determine the effects it has, if released.

Table 5: Shareholder Communication

Measures/Activities	Objectives
• using new technology and media in addition to traditional to communicate • listening, processing, responding to concerns • informing about all current and planned measures/activities and their objectives • informing about strategic and operational considerations	• reaching both current and potential shareholders • creating environment to develop and nurture relationship with shareholders • obtaining support from current shareholders for strategic and operational decisions • attracting those shareholders that match the target firm's preferences

4. Research

(See table 6.)

Measures and activities as part of the research investment focus on basic and applied research. Experimental development is not considered in this context because it is an integrative part of one particular development process in the view of the author.

Table 6: Research

Measures/Activities	Objectives
• basic and applied research in general fields of technological and scientific interest	• providing ideas and contributing to ideas for innovations • obtaining information to forecast and evaluate technologies • increasing competencies and absorptive capacity in general fields of technological and scientific interest • preparing for quick innovations • helping to solve scientific and technological problems with regard to innovations

5. Capability to focus development

(See table 7.)

Several writers propose that the development process should not be separated from other organisational activities and processes in order to for it to be effective (McIlveen, 1994; Herbig and Palumbo, 1996; Ahmed, 1998; Rothwell, 1994; Mandeville, 1998). Therefore target firms' efforts with regard to development is best directed towards a capability to focus in order to increase effectiveness and efficiency. This capability stems in large parts from investments made in the other fields in the view of the author.[75]

Table 7: Capability to focus development

Measures/Activities	Objectives
• rigid project management which includes regular reviews and refocusing • other measures of focusing organisational structures towards development process	• generating knowledge about development and management methods from internal sources • processing of decision making about functionality, differentiation, compatibility, interfaces and modularity • processing of decision making about production and engineering issues • being able to revise decisions according to new knowledge • generating vision of what is needed • translating all available intelligence into most effective and efficient development process • controlling if vision and development process is adhered to

6. Organisational structures and culture

(See table 8.)

Organisational structures and culture comprise a variety of measures and infrastructure recommendations that all contribute to meeting the objectives of this investment. One can see the main purpose of this investment as being to create an organisational texture which has the potential to establish external links in order to realise all potential of the staff. All elements laid out in table 8 are relevant in their own right and only a continuous and cumulative effort will lead to the fulfilment of objectives according to their potential.[76]

[75] See section C.IV.7, p. 62

[76] The learning effect inherent in organisational structures and culture is a continuous process (see e.g. Swain, 1999)

Management has a tendency to avoid risk (Kuczmarski, 1996), in particular the management of target firms.[77] The measures proposed are based on the fact that continuous rethinking is necessary. However, one has to recognise that the management of target firms cannot be expected to continually make decisions of high risk. That is the reason why organisational structures and culture are necessary to play the important role of raising internal intelligence and disseminating it to where it is needed, specifically management. One could argue that the more effectively this is achieved the less risky management decisions become.[78]

Table 8: Organisational structures and culture

Measures/Activities and Infrastructure	**Objectives**
• modern information technology for intelligence/ knowledge management • information technology that is compatible to create inter-organisational links • creating architectural spaces where informal communication between staff is possible and encouraged • regular communication through links between business units (personal and via technology) • training and encouraging the use of technology forecasting techniques and other information sharing and discussion techniques,[79] independently and formalised • employing only skilled staff who would fit into the culture • job rotation programs • advanced manufacturing technology • other total quality management measures • establishing policies to foster and reward the use communication techniques • establishing policies to foster and reward creativity and the processing of intelligence • the management plays an active part in the organisational culture and allows the staff to be heard and ideas to be considered in personal as well as formal ways	• fostering creativity • absorbing, filtering and processing intelligence • communicating and disseminating intelligence • making use of all expertise and potential of staff • being able to gather internal intangible knowledge and disseminating it • making processed organisational intelligence tangible • enabling intelligence to be used more effectively and efficiently • intelligence risk diversification • crossing functional and hierarchical barriers • having the ability to cross inter-organisational boundaries • supporting management functions in decision making • achieving decision flexibility • continuity in improvement effort • learning about effectiveness and efficiency of other investments, in particular competitive intelligence • building competencies and absorptive capacity • forecasting and evaluating technology • integrating other investments

[77] See section B.II.2, p. 28

[78] Security issues arise as more information is made available to staff (Attaway, 1998). However, the benefits of organisational structures and culture as described outweigh security problems, in the view of the author. See sections C.IV.7, p. 62 and C.IV.8, p. 66

[79] See Lemos and Porto (1998) and Attaway (1998)

7. Interdependencies

In order to assess the investments one can now estimate the interdependencies between them. To achieve a certain level of clarity, only the direct interdependencies are considered, i.e. if the *measures* of one investment *directly* influence the effectiveness and efficiency of measures of another.[80] It would not be beneficial to understanding if indirect interdependencies were included in the figures. In the explanations and subsequently in figure 13 the following acronyms are used to refer to the investments:

- Competitive Intelligence **CI**
- Competitive Support and Education **CSE**
- Shareholder Communication **SC**
- Research **R**
- Capability to focus development **CFD**
- Organisational structures and culture **OSC**

Competitive intelligence

Intelligence gathering and processing does influence the performance potential of CSE as some of the information will be passed back to the environment. There is a similar effect on SC, however less of it is direct. Gathered information can point out in which fields and how thoroughly to conduct research. CI can be considered essential to be able to focus the development process. It exhibits medium interdependencies with OSC because CI enforces communication and inspires to be creative. Generally, CI contributes significantly to other investments and it effects all fields.

Competitive support and education

As part of their CSE activities, target firms, gather information in an effective and efficient way, as they have direct contact with the objects of observation. CSE therefore enables the target firms to 'test' their intelligence data and therefore to enhance evaluation and decision making. Therefore, target firms can significantly increase their CFD. Research and OSC are also influenced by the ability to

[80] If the effectiveness and efficiency of one investment is directly influenced by the performance increase of another investment which has been induced by the measures of a third investment, one can view this interdependency as indirect.

evaluate information and decide, however to a lesser extend. CSE, therefore has a similar effect on other investments as CI. As CSE emphasises relationships rather than information gathering and processing, its contributions have a slightly different focus. Generally, CSE contributes to all other investments and overall in a relatively significant way.

Shareholder communication

Feedback of shareholders can provide a focus as to which development activities should be going on. In the view of the author, all other investments are less influenced by communication with the shareholder but rather by financial support which is not a direct interdependency. Its direct contribution is therefore limited with regard to strength and scope.[81]

Research

Research provides general information regarding technologies. It therefore teaches target firms what to look for in their CI efforts. The relation to CSE is indirect, mainly via CI. As research provides information to evaluate technologies the CFD, justifying decisions to shareholders and discussing and justifying internally are positively influenced. Generally, the direct contribution of research to other investments is limited, yet the scope of interdependencies is broad.

Capability to focus development

CFD contributes to CI, CSE and SC in the same way as research does. However, research contributes through intelligence whereas CFD contributes through being able to manage. The overall performance of investment in research is not directly dependent on the CFD, as the overall benefits of research do not necessarily increase when it is conducted with a strong focus.[82] If the target firm is able to focus its development processes, communication and spirit can be positively influenced. Overall, CFD does not directly contribute much to other investments and the scope of contribution is limited.

---

[81] The proposition that shareholder communication does not directly influence other investments does not lower the relevance in its own right.

[82] See section C.III.3.a, p. 47

Organisational structures and culture

As the goal of CI is to increase knowledge levels and to disseminate intelligence to where it is needed, OSC contributes significantly towards this investment. Moreover, intelligence gathering is a concerted activity the management of which OSC can support. Furthermore, OSC can help manage activities and information flow for CSE. Direct influence on SC mainly derives from the infrastructure that is part of the OSC investments, if large amounts of shareholders need to be dealt with. Research benefits from OSC when integration of research into the general intelligence flow is sought. Finally, OSC can be considered almost essential for achieving CFD. Generally, one can say that OSC contributes significantly with wide scope.

Figure 13: Direct interdependencies between investments

is contributed to \ *contributes*	CI	CSE	SC	R	CFD	OSC	*cum.*	*no. of other inv.* (*potential increase through other investments*)
CI	-	2		1	1	3	*7*	*4*
CSE	2	-				2	*4*	*2*
SC	1	1	-	1	1	1	*5*	*5*
R	2	1		-		1	*4*	*3*
CFD	3	3	1	2	-	3	*12*	*5*
OSC	2	1	.	1	1	-	*5*	*4*
cum.	*10*	*8*	*1*	*5*	*3*	*10*		
no. of other inv.	*5*	*4*	*1*	*4*	*4*	*5*		

potential increase of other investments

Legend: 1 low; 2 medium; 3 high

General remarks

The exact interdependencies as suggested above are debatable figures. Therefore, the author suggests two categorisations, one for cumulative interdependencies, the other for the scope of interdependencies. Cumulative values are translated into four categories with values from one to four, five to eight, nine to twelve and thirteen and above. For the number of other investments with direct interdependencies, three categories with values one to two, three to four and five will be used. Figure 14 depicts cumulative values from and towards investments and figure 15 shows the scope in the same manner.

Figure 14: Cumulative direct contribution to and from other investments

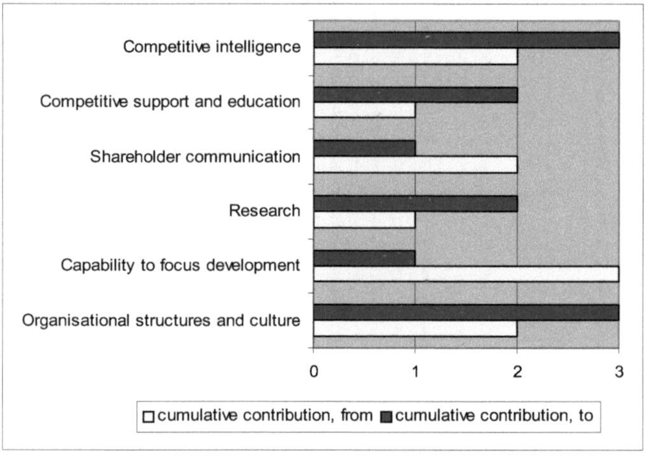

Figure 15: Direct contribution to and from number of investments

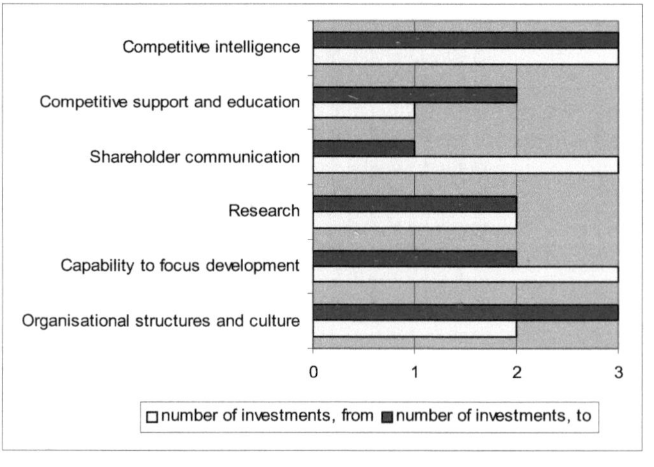

Notwithstanding the conclusion from above, one can say that CI, CSE and OSC are the main direct contributors, i.e. they contain the strongest direct interdependencies with other investments. At the same time, the performance of CFD is highly dependent on other investments.

8. Investment levels

The question that remains to be answered is how much target firms have to invest into each field in order to achieve the goal of staying competitive. As has been said initially, firms have to engage in all six fields. If one takes into account all the measures that these investments consist of, one can conclude that firms need a certain amount of economies of scale to be able to do so effectively and efficiently. Target firms' economies of scale and their ability to allocate funds have been identified as part of their strengths.

If one were to assess the cost levels of investments, one would have to examine specific target firms. From the measures suggested, one could argue that competitive intelligence, competitive support and education and organisational structures and culture are those that require relatively more resources than other investments. Furthermore as they contribute significantly to other investments, reducing the levels of these investments will have a larger impact on competitiveness.

The fact that measures and objectives of research are limited bases on the realisation that innovation can be achieved in by increasing knowledge in many different directions. Nevertheless, certain technologies may require costly machinery or a wide spectrum of research.[83] By defining clear objectives target firms can be certain in what way research contributes to competitiveness and are therefore better able to determine the level needed to avoid becoming non-competitive.[84]

The levels of shareholder communication and the capability to focus development are mainly influenced by synergy possibilities with other investments. Hence an increase in other investments leads to less costs for these investments.

[83] The scientific content of technological knowledge can be complex and important to the existence of a high technology. See section B.I.8, p. 19

[84] Schilling (1998) says that the deciding factor for the level of research needed is the minimum to avoid technological lockout.

Research seems to suggest that continuity is the most significant requirement for these investments. The main argument is the learning curve, i.e. that competencies which enable firms to achieve the investments goals effectively and efficiently are built up in the course of time.[85] Furthermore, there are many direct interdependencies between investments where one enhances the performance of the other. Hence, investments should be seen both for what their objectives are and for how they enhance others. This leads to the conclusion that continuous investment in all fields is the best way to increase the ability to sustain competitiveness.

[85] See Cohen and Levinthal (1990) concerning absorptive capacity, Bakker et al. (1994) concerning core competencies, Mintzberg (1998: 362-4) regarding organisational culture.

D. Corporate venture capital and competitiveness

I. Basics of corporate venture capital

1. Definition and differentiation

The term *corporate venture capital* (CVC) consists of the two elements *corporate* and *venture capital*. It implies that venture capital is given by corporations, i.e. large firms (McNally, 1997). As venture capital is usually issued to smaller, or small to medium sized companies, it is a form of collaboration between large and small firms.[86] It is generally agreed upon that in the case of CVC, the main business activities of investing corporations are not financial investments (McNally, 1997; Schween, 1996; Silver, 1993). Rather it is seen as an investment of limited quantity to complement other investments.

Firms can engage in a number of different activities in the context of new ventures. Figure 16 shows six recognised venture strategies for large firms. The fact that there are not only several strategies, but also different ways of achieving them has led to inconsistencies in the definition of CVC. The most common term used instead of CVC is corporate venturing (McNally, 1997). According to McNally corporate venturing denotes any activity that is intended to start and nurture new ventures of corporations. He differentiates internal and external corporate venturing. The former is an activity new to the organisation, of higher risk and uncertainty than other activities, which is conducted or initiated internally and managed separately at some time during its life (Block and MacMillan, 1993: 14, cited by McNally, 1997). Schween (1996) differentiates further into intrapreneuring and regular internal corporate venturing, the former being an internal motivation concept to promote entrepreneurial thinking, whereas the latter is a more formal, organisational approach. External corporate venturing "involves a structured relationship (...) [with] smaller, unquoted, usually innovative firms". (NEDO, 1986, cited by McNally, 1997: 37) of strategic purpose.[87] Hence it is does not necessarily involve equity investment by the larger company.[88]

[86] The main characteristics of venture capital according to Albach (1983, cited by Schween, 1996) are that a) it is an equity stake in new, high-growth or small to medium sized enterprises, b) it is accompanied by managerial support by the giving entity, and c) investments are longer term and aimed at capital gain
[87] According to McNally (1997: 37), the term 'external corporate venturing' is used to describe all forms of strategic partnerships between large and small firms.
[88] However, equity stake is often used to complement the strategic partnership (McNally, 1997).

Figure 16: Spectrum of venture strategies

1	2	3	4	5	6
Venture capital	**Venture nurturing**	**Venture spin-off**	**New style joint venture**	**Venture merging and melding**	**Internal venture**

low corporate involvement/ risk ....→ high corporate involvement/ risk

| .... External .... | Internal

Key

1 Large firm investment of capital in stock of small company
2 As above but also incorporates managerial assistance for the small firm
3 Large company spins-off a new business as a separate firm with financial support
4 Large and small firms enter jointly into new ventures
5 Combination of venture strategies so far
6 Development of an 'in-house' entrepreneurial unit

Source: McNally (1997: 34, adapted from Roberts, 1980: 136)

Corporate venture capital denotes a minority equity stake in small, unquoted companies by corporations as outlined above. (McNally, 1997).[89] The investees are legally independent entities (Schween, 1996). Objectives of CVC investments are not limited to *strategic* concerns, they can also be of *financial* or *social* nature.[90] McNally (1997: 43) also identifies *learning about venture capital* as an objective. Section D.II.1 describes these objectives in more detail.

2. Types and internal organisation of CVC investment

Corporate venture capital investment can be made indirectly or directly. Concerns can invest indirectly via independently managed venture capital funds or directly in specific firms (see figure 17). Independently managed funds can either be pooled funds in which money from target firms and other institutional investors[91] is invested or captive, client-based funds where the target firm is the only

[89] Schween (1996) postulates that a vital element of CVC is that the corporation provides managerial support. This is typical of CVC investments as is the provision of other resources or the corporation's reputation, however not constituent, as outlined by Hurry *et al.* (1992) for Japanese corporations.
[90] Social reasons are those that can be described as being derived from social responsibility of large concerns. In the view of the author, social reasons are at least partially of strategic nature, as there is a potential positive influence on public relations.
[91] E.g. pension funds and insurance companies.

investor.[92] In the latter case the investor has considerable influence over the choice of investees. In addition to actual investments of both types, target firms can engage in venture nurturing and the formation of further strategic partnerships with investees. If investments are done indirectly the investors has less contact and influence with regard to the investee.[93]

Figure 17: Types and internal organisation of corporate venture capital investment

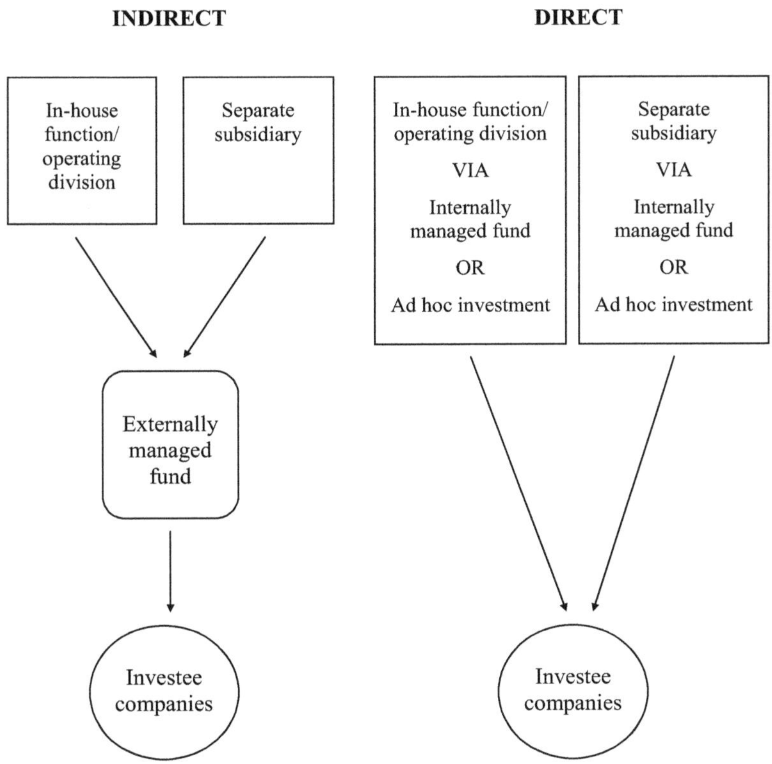

Source: McNally (1997: 108)

[92] For both fund types, the portfolio can be structured as typical venture capital funds or focused on specific groups of small companies (Schween, 1996).

[93] According to Schween (1996: 121, 124-130) investors can seek contact via participation in advisory boards. He only considers direct investments for investors that want to engage in venture nurturing activities. He adds that venture spin-offs and new style joint venture are other typical cases of direct investments.

Irrespective of the type, target firms can organise CVC investment activities as an in-house function or in a separate subsidiary. Furthermore the management of direct investments by target firms can be accomplished via an internally managed fund[94] or as ad-hoc, one-off investments. Likewise, the level of contact and influence varies. It mainly depends on internal structures, i.e. autonomy of fund management and subsidiary, the flow of information and how interested and involved the management of the investor is.

3. Characteristics of the investment process

The characteristics presented are based on empirical findings and discussions in the two studies by McNally (1997) for the UK and Schween (1996) for Germany, as they are the most detailed ones. The study by Hurry *et al.* (1992) for Japan and the US is used to provide additional information.

Research regarding CVC is limited. The available empirical data show that characteristics are not uniform. However, empirical data can provide an insight into the investment process. Generally, one can conclude from the studies that investors in the UK, Japan and Germany have primarily long-term strategic objectives, whereas objectives of US investors are more balanced between financial and strategic objectives.

a. Finding suitable investments

Funds are selected according to their type and focus as well as the management experience and track records of the fund managers. McNally (1997: 110-111) found out that investors with strategic objectives place additional emphasis on the focus on particular sectors or development stages of investees, whereas investors with social objectives prefer a regional focus. The objective of learning about venture capital leads to less preferences whereas financial objectives result in the critical assessment of all possible criteria, including the sizes of investments in investees.

Candidates for direct investments are sought via continual scanning or intermediaries.[95] Sometimes they are chosen because of previous relationships or because they have approached the investors.[96] Investments can be done collateral with venture capitalists, as spin-offs or as new style joint ventures (McNally,

[94] Similar to captive, client-based funds.
[95] E.g. accountants, lawyers, consultants, merchant banks and venture capitalists or other sources such as universities, research institutions and customers.

1997: 111-112, Schween, 1996: 105). In the UK study, technologies, products and markets of investees were the most important criteria. The management of investees is less important than for regular venture capitalists. Those having social objectives identified the management team as being more important and those with primarily financial objectives said that all possible criteria are equally important. In the US and Germany, the management team generally has been identified as being more important than in the UK.[97] Furthermore, in the UK, the approval process of direct investments is more rigid than for indirect investments. Autonomy in the investment approval process is explained with the lack of strategic objectives (McNally, 1997: 111-2).

b. *Portfolios*

In the UK, investment in funds range from GBP25,000 to GBP15m with typical values between GBP2m and GBP5m. Investments for social reasons tend to be smaller. The number of investees per fund range up to 50 and investments per venture are less than the average venture capital investment.[98] Funds provide predominantly early stage finance for investees. Sizes of direct investments vary considerably.[99] They concentrate on expansion rather than early stage financing.[100] The other studies do not provide detailed data.

In the UK a large portion of the investees of funds are located in the US whereas those of direct investments tend to be in the UK. Most investees of German investors are located in the US.[101] The average number of direct investees per investor in the UK lies between seven and eight, a smaller range than via funds. Figures regarding Japanese and US investors are not clear as there is no differentiation between funds and direct investments. However Japanese firms tend to invest smaller amounts in a larger number of companies than US investors (Hurry *et al.*, 1992: 91).

c. *Maintaining investments*

The frequency of communication with fund managers varies greatly among investors. It ranges from daily to once a year. Typical frequencies are monthly or

---

96 In the study by McNally (1997) only few investors had been approached by fund seeking firms.
97 The difference to regular venture capitalists is still evident, however.
98 60% of investments are less than GBP0.5m (McNally, 1997: 121)
99 In the UK from GBP30,000 to GBP7m. There are similar ranges in Japan, whereas in the US, investments are larger by average.
100 Due to the fact that the number of new direct investments has declined towards the end of the study, this figure can be distorted.

quarterly, with the exception of the Japanese who only review their investments twice a year. McNally (1997: 113-4) states that initial communication emphasises fund management policies whereas later only performance and management updates are sought. The contact to investees is limited and there is barely any nurturing.

Direct investments are usually monitored closely with the exception of the Japanese who review their direct investments as frequent as their indirect investments. Usually investors take seats in the board of most investees and engage in nurturing activities.

d. Developing investments and divesting

According to Schween (1996: 105) it is typical to employ milestones to plan the development of a venture. Upon passing a milestone, further finance is provided. The investor can give loan capital to keep the minority status and obtain support from co-investors. The involvement as a corporate venture capital investor ends when the venture has better access to other funds, e.g. via the stock market. The investor can then sell out or acquire the venture (Schween, 1996: 115).

Direct investments lead to significantly more strategic partnerships than indirect investments (McNally, 1997: 114-5). In former research it has remained uncertain whether direct or indirect investments provide better opportunities for strategic objectives. It has been suggested that a double strategy can optimise strategic benefits (McNally, 1997: 44). For Japanese investors, it is the primary goal to establish contractual agreements for large scale commercialisation after a venture has proven to be initially successful.[102] However, the US investors' primary aim is to divest to realise the capital gain.

II. Corporate venture capital investment and sustaining competitiveness

1. Potential benefits of corporate venture capital investment

Both Silver (1993)[103] and McNally (1997)[104] compile detailed lists of objectives for corporate venture capital investment as they were given and subsequently

[101] The study does not differentiate between funds and direct investments in this issue.
[102] Hurry *et al.* (1992) describe the investment as an option on technology which is exercised if the venture is successful.
[103] A study of approximately 100 US corporate venture capitalists.
[104] A study of 73 UK based corporations.

ranked by companies that are active as investors. Schween (1996)[105] provides a shorter list which was included in his survey to be ranked. These objectives resemble potential benefits which can be derived from CVC investment. The following three tables show the objectives as they were given and ranked.

Table 9: Objectives of CVC investment as identified by Silver

Objective	Rank
To incubate and reduce cost of acquisition	1
Exposure to possible new markets	2
Add new products	3
A less expensive form of R&D	4
To expose middle management to entrepreneurship	5
Training for junior management	6
Utilise excess plant space, time and people	7
To mesh activities of several departments	8
To generate capital gain	9
Develop antennae for new technologies	10
Income generating	11
Group therapy senior management	12
Good public relations	13
The competition may be doing it	14
To retain a stake in spin-offs	15
To encourage new company formation in the community	16

Source: adapted from Silver (1993, cited by McNally, 1997: 42-3)

Table 10: Objectives of CVC investment as identified by Schween

Objective	Rank
Observe technologies and markets	1
Generate innovations	2
Identify and assess potential acquistion candidates	3
Develop business relationships	4
Learn about venture capital	5
Financial return	6
Assist spin-offs	7
Need to become more entrepreneurial, change corporate culture	8
Support of regional economy	9

Source: adapted from Schween (1996: 242)

105 A study of 12 German corporations.

Table 11: Objectives of CVC investment as identified by McNally

Objective	Rank Primary	Rank Secondary
Identify new markets	1	8
Exposure to new technologies	2	11
Financial return	3	1
Develop business relationships	4	3
Identify new products	5	11
Improve manufacturing processes	6	8
Identify and assess potential acquisition candidates	7	5
Learn about venture capital	8	8
Lower manufacturing costs	8	5
Social responsibility	8	14
Help suppliers/customers	11	5
Indirect benefit from enhanced small firm sector	12	3
Publicity for company	12	-
Assist spin-offs	12	14
Assure continued supply of materials/components	15	11
Need to become more entrepreneurial, change corporate culture	-	1

Source: adapted from McNally (1997: 87). Rank primary denotes the rank as a primary objective, rank secondary denotes the rank as a secondary objective.

As one can see certain objectives are similar in all studies. In order to assess objectives more easily, one can categorise them. The author suggests the categories as they are presented in table 12.[106]

Hurry *et al.* (1992) state that the objective of Japanese investors is obtaining an option on new technologies rather than investing for a direct return. As described in the section before, if a technology is successful, Japanese firms either acquire the venture or establish a contractual relationship to commercialise it.[107] This strategy comprises objective categories A, C, D and H. Furthermore, Hurry *et al.* reason that Japanese firms achieve these objectives because they make small investments in a large number of companies to ensure that at least some options are successful. US firms which put more emphasis on financial gain make larger and more selective investments.

106 If it is clear that certain objectives are equal they are only mentioned once.

107 Hence the investor has a fixed risk. The success of this strategy contradicts the 'acquire all or leave alone' approach by UK firms as described by McNally (1997: 69)

Table 12: Categories of objectives

A) Observe technologies and markets	Identify new markets Exposure to possible new markets Exposure to new technologies Identify new products Identify and assess potential acquisition candidates Develop antennae for new technologies
B) Change corporate culture	Expose middle management to entrepreneurship Training for junior management Mesh activities of several departments Group therapy senior management Become more entrepreneurial
C) Grow	Add new products Generate innovations
D) Economise	To incubate and reduce cost of acquisition A less expensive form of R&D Improve manufacturing processes Utilise excess plant space, time and people Lower manufacturing costs
E) Financial	Generate capital gain Income generating
F) Social	Social responsibility Indirect benefits from enhanced small firm sector Support of regional economy Encourage new company formation in the community
G) Public relations	Publicity for company
H) Control	Develop business relationships Help suppliers and customers Assist spin-offs Retain a stake in spin-offs Assure continued supply of materials and components
I) Learning	Learn about venture capital The competition may be doing it

Regarding *category A*, one can say that the *new market* objectives for target firms are mainly concerned with new core technologies and market segments[108] and not with geographical markets.[109] If one considers the rankings, one can say that observing new core technologies and their market segments is a very important objective. The results of the studies by McNally (1997) and Schween (1996) suggest that this objective has generally been achieved satisfactorily. The UK study shows that direct investments are more effective than indirect investments.

[108] See section B.II.4, p. 32

[109] Schween (1996: 84) notes that target firms usually have satisfactory means available to develop distribution channels and hence do not need CVC for this.

Furthermore, the *identification of acquisition candidates* and subsequent acquiring (categories C and D) is significant as this is a feasible investment strategy.

Category B mainly consists of objectives given by US investors. The German study shows that, even though few investors had these objectives, the ones that did achieved them very satisfactorily (Schween, 1996: 242). UK investors see category B as a very important secondary objective, however do not report the results to be adequate. Direct investments achieved slightly better results than indirect investments (McNally, 1997: 130). One can say that the benefits of this category are not certain and may depend on other circumstances.

Objectives of US, German and Japanese investors comprise *category C*. Hurry *et al.* (1992) suggest that Japanese firms achieve very positive results. German investors rate the objective as being fulfilled only to a very limited extent. One could argue that a wider dispersion of CVC investment increases opportunities for growth. *Category D* primarily consists of objectives that are complementary to categories A and C The objectives mentioned in the UK study, i.e. *improve manufacturing process* and *lower manufacturing costs*, were fulfilled to a limited extend with direct investments.

Category E is mentioned as an important objective in all studies, in the UK and German studies, however only as an important secondary aim. The objectives were not achieved very satisfactorily with the exception of US investors as mentioned by Hurry *et al.* (1992) and Siegel *et al.* (1988: 242). Hurry *et al.* also say that Japanese investors do not expect any direct returns from the investment. However once a venture is commercialised on a large scale as described above, the primary objective becomes financial. Schween (1996: 88-9) states that strategic and financial objectives are not compatible. He argues that strategic objectives and financial objectives each lead to different initial investment selections. Even though research is not clear about the compatibility of strategic and financial objectives (McNally, 1997: 43) the studies indicate that strategic objectives eventually lead to financial gains which are, however, not directly induced by capital gain from the investments.

Even though the importance of *categories F and G* is limited, both were rated as satisfactory by UK investors with the exception of indirect benefits from enhanced small firm sector.[110] The German study depicted a low performance of

[110] Category F performed better with direct investments and category G was only rated by companies with indirect investments.

category F. However, as McNally (1997: 212-3) concludes the low rating of indirect investment may reflect overdrawn expectations.

The performance of *category H* is perceived as positive, however only for direct investments. Investors have rated the *development of business relationships* and *helping suppliers and customers* as successful. The former has also been rated as important in all studies whereas the latter is considered as a secondary objective merely in the UK study.[111] *Spin-off* financing is considered to be less important. The UK investors rate the performance as highest among all objectives for direct investments. Indirect investment is not suitable for spin-off support. The German study rated the performance as lower, however the standard deviation of the appraisal is high. In both the UK and the German studies, *category I* is rated as well achieved.[112]

Generally, McNally (1997: 212) has found that all objectives have at least been fulfilled satisfactorily with direct investments. He also notes that the performance of indirect investments has not been rated as high as those of direct investments for all objectives.[113] Social objectives, publicity objectives, financial objectives and learning objectives are the only ones to be rated satisfactory for indirect investments. Furthermore, achieving high financial performance directly by the investment cannot be secured unless the investment portfolio is specifically aimed at capital gain. Financial benefits are mainly derived indirectly via achieving other objectives. Lastly, CVC investment lowers the risk and reduces the cost of acquisition and therefore facilitates the achievement of long-term growth.

2. Potential problems of corporate venture capital investment

McNally (1997), Schween (1996) and Siegel *et al.* (1988) have observed a range of problems CVC investors have to deal with. Even though the weighting by the investors is not uniform for all reported problems, the range of criticisms is similar. Primary concerns are inadequate deal flow, finding appropriate investment management, conflicting objectives between parties,[114] lack of

[111] *Assuring supply* can be seen as complementary to *helping suppliers*.
[112] Satisfaction was highest of all objectives in the German study. In the study by McNally fulfilment was rated highest of all indirect investment and among the first three for direct investments.
[113] McNally states that companies making indirect investments stopped their CVC activities because objectives were not met whereas reasons for direct investors to cease activities are unrelated to the performance. Also see Schween (1996: 197).
[114] Internal investment management, external fund management, executives of investors, management of investees.

understanding between parties, lack of autonomy of internal investment management from board of executives, underestimating the risk of investment, lack of clear mission and objectives and incompatible cultures of investor and investee (McNally, 1997:131-3; Schween, 1996: 193-200; Siegel *et al.*, 1988: 239).[115]

McNally (1997: 27-30) finds that a number of problems concerning the relationship between investor and investee are typical of strategic partnerships between large and small firms. The most significant problems are the lack of trust between employees and the failure to move towards each other concerning values and perceptions. McNally states that problems could be solved if firms strengthened communication and commitment.

A problem specifically related to German investors is divesting. Schween notes that the cause for this circumstance may be inflexible regulations of the German capital market. Hence this potential problem should be limited to German investees.[116] Furthermore, as said above, divesting is only one strategy for CVC investment.

Generally, investors have expressed that most obstacles can be overcome by experience (McNally, 1997: 133, Siegel *et al.* 1988: 243). Inexperienced investors are said to have inappropriate expectations. Moreover, the lack of mission and concrete objectives for CVC investment, which is seen as significant problem, should become less critical with experience. McNally observes that many investors who report certain problems to be critical still engage in CVC investment.

3. How benefits and problems relate to competitive investments

In chapter C, the author has developed an approach for target firms to sustain competitiveness. The investments in six fields as outlined in C.IV, which will subsequently be called *competitive investments*, are similar in some aspects to CVC investments. In the following section the relation between CVC investment and competitive investments will be shown. Objective categories and distinct objectives to denote the benefits as described above are taken from table 11.

One can say that objectives of the category *observe technologies and markets* are directly related to competitive intelligence. The evidence that these

[115] Some of the problems between parties have their roots in the principle-agent relationship (Schween, 1996: 138-147).

objectives can be achieved, specifically via direct CVC, underlines the effectiveness of CVC as a competitive intelligence investment.

Control benefits as well as *public relations* and *social* benefits of CVC can be seen as similar to parts of investments in competitive support and education. The objectives *developing business relationships* as well as *helping customers and suppliers*[117] and *spin-off support*, shown as being achievable via direct CVC, can be seen as a part of competitive support and education. Social and public relation benefits may facilitate competitive support and education, primarily because the investor has a better public image. Competitive intelligence and shareholder communication are influenced in a similar way as they also involve contact and relationships with individuals or organisations outside of the target firm.

Investment in research can be complemented by the research and development which is carried out by CVC investees. The objective *a less expensive form of R&D* in the category *economise* hence could be seen as contributing to the research investment if scientific and technological knowledge is transferred from investee to investor. Yet, there is no empirical evidence of how well this objective has been achieved. Hence this relation is less certain than those mentioned before.

The objectives of the category *change corporate culture* are directly part of the investment in organisational structures and culture. As described above cultural benefits of CVC investments are not certain and may depend on other circumstances. If one takes into account that direct investments achieved better result and the problems that have been outlined for large firm - small firm collaboration, one could argue that cultural benefits of CVC investment can be increased if there is more contact and communication between employees. The objectives *improve manufacturing process*, *lower manufacturing costs* and *utilise excess plant space, time and people* can also be considered as part of before-mentioned competitive investment. However, the overall contribution is limited as the investment in organisational structures and culture comprises a wide range of measures.

---

[116] German companies have primarily made investments in US firms.
[117] This objective is complementary to the objective *assure supply*.

Table 13: Potential contribution of CVC investment to competitive investments

Competitive Investments	CVC Investment Objective	Category	Relation
Competitive intelligence	Identify new markets	Observe technologies and markets	*part of*
	Exposure to new markets		
	Exposure to new technologies		
	Identify new products		
	Identify and assess potential acquisition candidates		
	Develop antennae for new technology		
	Social responsibility	Social	*facilitate*
	Indirect benefits from enhanced small firm sector		
	Support of regional economy		
	Encourage new company formation in the community		
	Publicity for company	Public relation	
Competitive support and education	Develop business relationships	Control	*part of*
	Help suppliers and customers		
	Assist spin-offs		
	Retain a stake in spin-offs		
	Assure continued supply of materials and components		
	Social responsibility	Social	*facilitate*
	Indirect benefits from enhanced small firm sector		
	Support of regional economy		
	Encourage new company formation in the community		
	Publicity for company	Public relation	
Shareholder communication	Social responsibility	Social	*facilitate*
	Indirect benefits from enhanced small firm sector		
	Support of regional economy		
	Encourage new company formation in the community		
	Publicity for company	Public relation	
Research	A less expensive form of R&D	Economise	*part of*
Organisational structures and culture	Expose middle management to entrepreneurship	Change corporate culture	*part of*
	Training for junior management		
	Mesh activities of several departments		
	Group therapy senior management		
	Become more entrepreneurial		
	Improve manufacturing processes	Economise	
	Utilise excess plant space, time and people		
	Lower manufacturing costs		

The remaining objective categories, i.e. *grow*, *financial* and *learning* and the objective *incubate and reduce cost of acquisition* do not directly contribute to competitive investments. Financial and growth objectives including reduced costs of acquisitions can be seen as a replacement for innovation and value creating efforts of target firms. If target firms are not able to use all of their resources to become innovative, they buy competitiveness with successful ventures. Learning about venture capital on the other hand is an important objective which is needed to achieve other objectives satisfactorily. As has been outlined concerning problems with CVC investments, learning is necessary to overcome them.

Furthermore, taking into account the organisational and informational nature of most problems, one can say that CVC investment requires additional strength of target firms in the field of organisational structures and culture, competitive intelligence and competitive support and education. One could argue that it depends on experience whether CVC investment takes away more from competitive investments than it contributes.

4. Conclusions about CVC investment and sustaining competitiveness

In chapter C, it has been recognised that target firms need current competitiveness and the ability to sustain competitiveness. From a detailed discussion following the framework given by Feuer and Chaharbaghi (1994), the author has concluded that competitive investments, i.e. continuous investment in six fields as outlined, increase the target firms' ability to sustain competitiveness by knowing where to direct resources and by being able to do so in order to realise competitiveness in given circumstances.

The relation of CVC investment to competitive investment as outlined above shows that CVC investment can only contribute in part to the ability to sustain competitiveness. The most direct contributions are technology and market observation benefits, control benefits and corporate culture benefits. If these benefits are related to the extent of the competitive investments to which are contributed, it becomes evident that CVC investment can only be seen as complementary. The scope of competitive investments goes beyond what can be achieved by CVC investment. With regard to the control benefits and the observation of technology and markets one can say that the scope achieved by CVC investment is limited to companies which are CVC candidates.

The contribution of CVC investment to the competitive investment *organisational structures and culture* can be effective if the potential of CVC investment is put in its proper place. From the above considerations, it becomes evident that CVC investment can only provide additional motivation and inspiration to the staff. One could argue that target firms must invest extensively in organisational structures and culture beforehand for the CVC investment benefit to be effective. Furthermore, the problems outlined indicate that target firms should provide frequent contact with investees to foster trust and communication.

The contribution of CVC investments to research is not certain. There may be some transfer of scientific and technological knowledge which otherwise would have to be gained via research. However, Cohen and Levinthal (1990) say that research is most effective if carried out internally. Hence the benefit *less expensive from of research and development* seems to primarily aim at generating innovation externally and can be seen in the same sense as the growth benefits.

Figure 18: Competitive investments and corporate venture capital investment

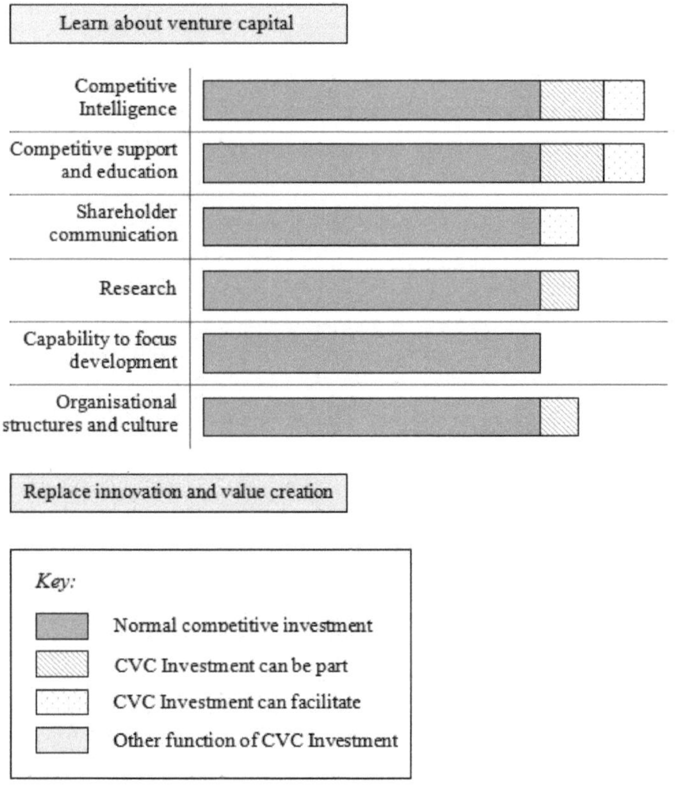

The learning objective can be seen as a critical element for CVC investment to be effective. An efficient way to achieve learning is indirect CVC investment as target firms gain knowledge from the external fund management and have access to a larger network of other investors. However, in order to achieve strategic benefits that contribute more to competitive investments, target firms eventually have to invest directly.

The composition of the CVC investment portfolio, i.e. the selection and the number of investees, has an impact on the effectiveness and the efficiency with which competitive investments are contributed to. From CVC investments of Japanese firms one can learn that a large number of small investments raises the effectiveness of the contribution to competitive intelligence and competitive support and education.[118] However, the efficiency of such a strategy must be questioned as the Japanese investors' primary concern is growth. Furthermore, if target firms have carried out comprehensive competitive investments, the investee selection process may improve. This in turn could reduce the number of investments needed to achieve the same effectiveness.

The question whether CVC investment is an efficient means of achieving above contribution to competitive investments remains to be answered. Direct financial benefits from CVC investment are not secured as shown above. If a large number of CVC investments do not lead to financial benefits, the contributions to competitive investments may become too expensive. It has been recognised, however, that venture capital finance creates employment at relatively low costs (Böndel and Dürand, 1995: 84, cited by Schween, 1996). Furthermore, some characteristics of the CVC investment contributions may not be achievable by efforts of target firms. One can conclude that target firms must specify the objectives to be achieved by CVC clearly to then decide whether CVC investment is the appropriate and efficient instrument.

This paper has investigated into how CVC investment can be seen in relation to the efforts of diversified high-technology concerns to stay competitive.

[118] The contributions to organisational culture cannot be increased significantly by a raising the number of investees over a certain level, in the view of the author. Whether the impact on organisational structure can be improved in this manner is questionable.

To sum up, one can say that the part of CVC is comparatively small one. However, CVC investment can provide certain elements with regard to competitive investments which may not be achievable internally. High technology concerns must determine clearly beforehand in which way CVC investment is to contribute to their competitiveness. Otherwise, funds may be better allocated to other undertakings.

Bibliography

Abell, D.F. (1978) 'Strategic Windows', *Journal of Marketing*, 7, p. 21

Ahern, R. (1993) 'The role of strategic alliances in the international organisation of industry', *Environment and Planning*, 25, pp. 1229-1246

Ahmed, P.K. (1998) 'Benchmarking innovation best practice', *Management & Technology*, 5: 1, pp. 45-58

Albach, H. (1983) *Zur Versorgung der Deutschen Wirtschaft mit Risikokapital*, ifm-Materialien Nr. 9, Institut für Mittelstandsforschung, Bonn

Anon (1993) *Handwörterbuch der Betriebswirtschaft* (5th ed), Wiesbaden, Gabler

Arthur, W.B. (1994) *Increasing returns and path dependency in the economy*, Ann Arbor, The University of Michigan Press

Attaway, M.C. (1998) 'A review of issues related to gathering and assessing competitive intelligence', *American Business Review*, 16: 1, pp. 25-35

Bakker, H., Jones, W. and Nichols, M. (1994) 'Using core competencies to develop new business', *Long Range Planning*, 27: 6, pp. 13-27

Banks, E. (1999) 'Creating a knowledge culture', *Work Study*, 48: 1, pp. 18-20

Basadur, M. (1995) *The Power of Innovation*, London, Pitman

Betz, F. (1987) *Managing Technology*, Englewood Cliffs, NJ, Prentice Hall

Betz, F. (1998) *Managing Technological Innovation - Competitive Advantage from Change*, New York, John Wiley & Sons

Block, Z. and MacMillan, I.C. (1993) *Corporate Venturing: Creating New Businesses within the Firm*, Boston, MA, Harvard Business School Press

Böndel, B. and Dürand, D. (1995) 'Risikokapital - Reich und berühmt', *Wirtschaftswoche*, 36, p. 78

Bowden, P. (1998) 'A practical path to customer loyalty', *Managing Service Quality*, 8: 4, pp. 248-255

Braun, C.F.v. (1997) *The Innovation War*, Upper Saddle River, NJ, Prentice Hall

Budworth, D.W. (1996) *Finance and Innovation*, International Thompson Business Press

Chaharbaghi, K. and Lynch, R. (1999) 'Sustainable competitive advantage: towards a dynamic resource-based strategy', *Management Decision*, 37: 1, pp. 45-50

Chattel, A. (1998) *Creating Value in the digital era*, London, Macmillan

Chen, I.J. and Small M.H. (1996) 'Planning for advanced manufacturing technology', *International Journal of Operations & Production Management*, 16: 5, pp. 4-24

Child, J. (1987) 'Information technology, organization, and the response to strategic challenges', *Californian Management Review*, Fall, pp. 33-50

Cohen, W.M. and Levinthal, D.A. (1990) 'Absorptive capacity: a new perspective on learning and innovation', *Administrative Science Quarterly*, 35: 1, pp. 128-153

Donath, B. (1997) 'Marketers of technology make promises they can't keep', *Marketing News*, 31: 21, pp. 5-6

Eden, Y. and Ronen, B. (1993) 'The declining-price paradox of new technologies', *Omega*, 21: 3, pp. 345-352

Feurer, R. and Chaharbaghi, K. (1994) 'Defining competitiveness: a holistic approach', *Management Decision*, 32: 2, pp. 49-58

Freeman, C. (1988) 'Diffusion: the spread of new technology to firms, sectors and nations', in Heertje, A. (ed) *Innovation, Technology and Finance*, Oxford, Basil Blackwell

Gerke, B. and Grupp, H. (1994) *Innovationspotential und Hochtechnologie - Technologische Position Deutschlands im internationalen Wettbewerb*, Heidelberg, Germany

Gnyawali, D.R. and Grant, J.H. (1997) 'Enhancing corporate venture performance through organizational learning', *International Journal of Organizational Analysis*, 5: 1, pp. 74-98

Gold, B., Rosegger, G. and Boylan, M.G. (1980) *Evaluating Technological Innovations*, Lexington, MA, LexingtonBooks

Han, J.K. (1998) 'Market orientation and organizational performance: is innovation a missing link?', *Journal of Marketing*, 62: 4, pp. 30-46

Hariolf Group (1997) 'External effects as microeconomic determinant of innovation efficiency', *International Journal of the Economics of Business*, 4: 2, pp. 173-178

Herbig, P.A and Palumbo, F.A. (1996) 'Innovation - Japanese Style', *Industrial Management and Data Systems*, 5, pp. 11-20

Hodgson, G.M. (1998) 'Evolutionary and competence based theories of the firm', *Journal of Economic Studies*, 25: 1, pp. 25-56

Hurry, D., Miller, A.T and Bowman, E.H. (1992) 'Calls on High-Technology: Japanese exploration of Venture Capital Investments in the United States', *Strategic Management Journal*, 13, pp. 85-101

Jovanovic, B. and Nyarko, Y. (1996) 'Learning by doing and the choice of technology', *Econometrica*, 64: 6, pp. 64-70

Kandampully, J. and Duddy, R. (1999) 'Competitive advantage through anticipation, innovation and relationships', *Management Decision*, 37: 1, pp. 51-56

Kotler, P. (1992), *Marketing Management*, Prentice Hall

Kruegel, N.F. and Brazeal, D.V. (1994) 'Entrepreneurial potential and potential entrepreneurs', *Entrepreneurship: Theory and Practice*, 18: 3, pp. 91-105

Kuczmarski, T.D. (1996) 'What is innovation? The art of welcoming risk', *Journal of Consumer Marketing*, 13: 5, pp. 7-11

Kumar, U. and Kumar, V. (1992) 'Technological Innovation Diffusion: the Proliferation of Substitution Models and Easing the User's Dilemma', *IEEE Transcripts on Engineering Management*, 39: 2, pp. 158-168

Kwasnicki, W. (1996) *Knowledge, Innovation and Economy*, Cheltenham, Edward Elgar

Layton, E. (1977) 'Conditions of technological development' in Spiege-Rösing, I. and Solla Price, D. (eds) *Science, Technology and Society: a Cross-Disciplinary Perspective*, Sage

Layton, E.T. (1971) 'Mirror image twins: the communities of science and technology in nineteenth century America', *Technology and Culture*, 12

Lemos, A.D. and Porto, A.C. (1998) 'Technological forecasting techniques and competitive intelligence: tools for improving innovation process', *Industrial Management and Data Systems*, 7, pp. 330-337

Leonard-Barton, D. (1994) 'Implementation as Mutual Adaptation of technology', in Rhodes, E. and Wield, D. (eds) *Implementing New Technologies: Innovation and the Management of Technology* (2nd edn), Oxford, NCC Blackwell, pp. 401-421

Lowe, A. (1995) 'The basic social processes of entrepreneurial innovation', *International Journal of Entrepreneurial Behaviour*, 1: 2, pp. 54-76

Mackewicz & Partner (1997) *Venture Capital and Corporate Venture Capital - Financing alternatives for Innovative Start-ups and Young Technological Companies*, Study Mackewicz & Partner Management Consultants, Munich

Mandeville, T. (1998) 'An information economics perspective on innovation', *International Journal of Social Economics*, 25: 2,3,4, pp. 357-364

Mascitelli, R (1999) *The Growth Warriors: Creating Sustainable Global Advantage for America's Technology*, Reed Publishing

Matsuyama, K. (1999) 'Growing through cycles', *Econometrica*, 67: 2, pp. 335-347

McIlveen, H. (1994) 'Product Development and the Consumer: The Reality of Managing Creativity', *Nutrition & Food Science*, 6, pp. 26-30

McNally, K. (1997), *Corporate Venture Capital: Bridging the Equity Gap in the small business sector*, London, Routlegde

Meffert, H. (1991) *Marketing - Grundlagen der Absatzpolitik* (7th ed), Wiesbaden, Gabler

Mintzberg, H. (1998) 'Ideology and the Missionary Organization', in Mintzberg, H., Quinn, J.B. and Ghoshal, S. (eds) *The Strategy Process – Revised European Edition*, Hertfordshire, Prentice Hall

Nerney, C. (1998) 'The competitive intelligence edge', *Network World*, 9 November, p. 42

Niederkofler, M. (1989) *External Corporate Venturing: Strategic Partnerships for Competitive Advantage*, Dissertation Nr. 1105, Hochschule St. Gallen, St. Gallen

OECD (1984) *Science and Technology Indicators, Resources Devoted to R&D*, Paris, OECD

Patrick J. (1997) *How to develop successful new products*, Chicago, IL, NTC

Pavitt, K. (1994) 'What we know bout the strategic management of technology', in Rhodes, E. and Wield, D. (eds) *Implementing New Technologies: Innovation and the Management of Technology* (2nd edn), Oxford, NCC Blackwell, pp. 176-185

Pettigrew, A. and Whipp, R. (1991) *Managing change for Competitive Success*, Oxford, Blackwell Publishers

Pinnington, A. and Haslop, D. (1995) 'Team leader autonomy in new product development', *Management Decision*, 33: 9, pp. 5-11

Rhodes, E. and Wield, D. (1994) 'Technology, Innovation Theory and the Implementation Process', in Rhodes, E. and Wield, D. (eds) *Implementing New Technologies: Innovation and the Management of Technology* (2nd edn), Oxford, NCC Blackwell, pp. 76-95

Roberts, E.B. (1980) 'New ventures for corporate growth', *Harvard Business Review*, 58: 4, pp. 134-142

Rogers, E.M. (1983) *Diffusion of Innovations*, New York

Rothwell, R. (1992) 'Successful industrial innovation: critical factors for the 1990s', *R&D Management*, 22: 30, pp. 221-239

Rothwell, R. (1994) 'Towards the Fifth-Generation Innovation Process', *International Marketing Review*, 11: 1, pp. 7-31

Scarso, E. (1996) 'Timing the adoption of a new technology: an option based approach', *Management Decision*, 34: 2, pp. 41-49

Schilling, M.A. (1998) 'Technological lockout: an integrative model of the economic and strategic factors of driving technology success and failure', *Academy of Management Review*, 23: 2, pp. 267-85

Schumpeter, J.A. (1987) *Capitalism, Socialism and Democracy* (6th ed), London, Unwin

Schween, K. (1996) *Corporate Venture Capital: Risikokapitalfinanzierung deutscher Industrieunternehmen*, Wiesbaden, Gabler

Servatius, H.G. (1988) *New Venture Management - Erfolgreiche Lösungen von Innovationsproblemen für Technologie-Unternehmen*, Wiesbaden

Shan, W. (1990) 'An empirical analysis of organization strategies by intrepreneurial high-technology firms', *Strategic Management Journal*, 11, pp. 129-139

Siegel, R., Siegel, E. and MacMillan, I.C. (1988) 'Corporate venture capitalists: autonomy, obstacles and performance', *Journal of Business Venturing*, 3, pp. 233-247

Silver, D.A. (1993) *Strategic Partnering*, New York, McGraw-Hill

Solomon, S.D. (1993) 'Things the tortoise taught us', *Technology Review*, 96: 4, pp. 20-28

Staal, F. (1995) 'Concepts of science in Europe and Asia', *Interdisciplinary Science Reviews*, 20: 1, pp. 7-19

Sultan, F. (1999) 'Consumer preferences for forthcoming innovations: the case of high definition television', *Journal of Consumer Marketing*, 16: 1, pp. 24-41

Swain, P. (1999) 'Organisational learning: developing leaders to deal with continous change - a strategic human resource perspective', *The Learning Organization*, 6: 1, pp. 30-37

Teece, D.J. (1994) 'Capturing Value from Technological Innovation: Integration, Strategic Partnering, and Licensing Decisions', in Rhodes, E. and Wield, D. (eds) *Implementing New Technologies: Innovation and the Management of Technology* (2nd edn), Oxford, NCC Blackwell, pp. 129-140

Teece, D.J. and Pisano, G. (1994) 'The dynamic capabilities of firms: an introduction', *Industrial and Corporate Change*, 3: 3, pp. 537-556

Twiss, B. (1992), *Managing technological innovation* (4th ed), London, Pitman

Wheeler, D. and Sillanpää, M. (1998) 'Including the Stakeholders: The Business Case', *Long Range Planning*, 31: 2, pp. 201-210

Wieandt, A. (1994) *Die Entstehung, Entwicklung und Zerstörung von Märkten durch Innovationen*, Schriftenreihe der Wissenschaftlichen Hochschule für Unternehmensführung Koblenz, Forschung/20, Stuttgart

Williamson, M. (1999) 'The technology upside', *Global Finance*, 13: 2, p. 8

Williamson, O. (1975) *Markets and Hierarchies: Analysis and Antitrust Implications*, New York, Free Press/MacMillan

Declaration of authenticity – Abschlußerklärung

I hereby declare that this paper has been written without the help of others. I have only used the literature which appears in the bibliography. All quotes and restatements are referenced.

Ich erkläre hiermit, die vorgelegte Arbeit ohne fremde Hilfe verfaßt zu haben. Ich habe keine andere als die angegebene Literatur verwendet. Alle wörtlichen oder gedanklichen Übernahmen sind zitiert.

Coventry, 25 April 1999